ELEMENTS OF WOODCARVING

ELEMENTS OF WOODCARVING

Chris Pye

GUILD OF MASTER CRAFTSMAN PUBLICATIONS LTD

First published 2000 by

Guild of Master Craftsman Publications Ltd,

166 High Street, Lewes, East Sussex BN7 1XU

© Christopher J. Pye 2000

Reprinted 2003

All photographs by Christopher J. Pye except where otherwise stated

All drawings by Christopher J. Pye

ISBN 1 86108 108 1

Designed by Christopher Halls at Mind's Eye Design, Lewes

Set in Trajan and Goudy

Colour origination by Viscan Graphics (Singapore)

Printed and bound by Kyodo Printing (Singapore)

MEASUREMENTS

Although care has been taken to ensure that imperial measurements are true and accurate, they are only
conversions from metric. They have usually been rounded up or down to the nearest ⅛in, or to the nearest
convenient equivalent in cases where the metric measurements themselves are only approximate.

CONTENTS

FOR KARL AND GUDRUN VOGEL

ACKNOWLEDGEMENTS

It feels as if I have a large lily pad in my hand. On it there sits, like an unprepossessing frog, a pile of paper, drawings and photographs. I hand the lot over to my publishers, trusting to the particular talents of my editor Stephen Haynes and the aesthetic skills of the book designer Chris Halls. Somewhile later, and somehow magically, returns a handsome prince of a book of which I can be proud. And readers give me the credit for this! As the author I only had the frog, fine as it might have been in itself. The real trick is turning it into a prince, and I am very grateful to these two for work that is so often taken for granted.

Thanks to all those who have allowed me to use their work, or commissioned the pieces which appear in this book, especially Beryl Thompson, Dharmachari Vajranatha, Janne and Chris Tupper, Gert Riemlinger and Renate Vogel, Mick Botten, Paul Davies, Sue Sharp and Vivien Wallace.

Finally, thank you, as ever, to my wife and life-enhancing companion Karin Vogel for her support and perceptive criticisms during the writing of this book and of the articles which preceded it.

PREFACE

Some readers will recognize projects in this book as having appeared previously in *Woodcarving* and other magazines. However, what you are holding is not just a reissue of these articles in another guise. It certainly is a way of salvaging this material, but more importantly, I am re-presenting the projects, somewhat rewritten and added to, in a new context.

All my books are a response to issues that have arisen as I teach and think about woodcarving. As this is my fifth, I have made use of cross-referencing to my earlier books. This is partly because I do not want always to have to repeat myself from one book to another – with details of sharpening, for example – and partly because I see these books as all one anyway. So, my apologies to readers who do not have other books of mine; I hope what you find here will encourage you to read them.

CHAPTER ONE

INTRODUCTION

One of my jobs as a woodcarving teacher is to wander among students in a class and oversee their progress, trying to guide what they are doing and helping them achieve their aims. Problem-solving is my major occupation.

Woodcarving can be a demanding skill: pieces break off, the carving just 'doesn't look right', the grain belligerently tears, the tools don't cut; there is the problem of what to carve next, of getting 'stuck', trying to undo what has been done, finding wood missing from where it is needed... so many problems to solve (Fig 1.1).

Fig 1.1 *The worst end of the learning curve! A good idea – a snail sliding along the corner of a shelf – but it ran into problems: thin wood breaking across the grain, wood missing from where the shell should be, the attaching screw hole wrongly sited...*

My response to such 'problems' is always one of interrogation. What is going on here? What exactly is the issue? I bounce questions off the work as I try to perceive what is in front of me. My aim is to make the carving more conscious, the whole working process more 'up front' and available for inspection.

I have found that answers always appear through this approach. I have also come to realize that my questions – and my assessment of what is happening, and consequent suggestions – fall into three distinct categories. Firstly, I might be asking about the student's technical attitude to the carving – whether it is well-planned or not; or whether there is a better choice of carving tool, or it could be more keenly sharpened; or perhaps whether the student could handle it in a more profitable way. Secondly, I would be asking whether the choice of wood has created difficulties; or if the way in which the work is held makes it awkward to get at, and could be improved. Lastly, I ask about the design: whether it overtaxes the ability of the student; whether the design is suited to wood as a material; and, importantly, whether the student really knows what he or she is aiming to carve.

In fact, I began to realize that all such considerations and concerns fell within three main areas: **design**, **material** and **technique**.

By becoming more aware of these elements, first consciously and then unconsciously, I find that students acquire a key to analysing and championing their own work and progress. They begin to carve more competently, with more confidence, even more 'professionally'.

Let me briefly define what I have called the **three elements of woodcarving**, so as to be clearer about what we are discussing.

DESIGN

The design, is, by definition, the artistic structure of a woodcarving. The thought and intention of the carver are manifested through the material and the handling of the tools; in this way they are revealed in the finished carving (Figs 1.2 and 1.3). The design, in a way, is the idea, and may be anything from simple tool marks or lettering through to the complex high altars of Riemenschneider illustrated in Chapter 14 (Figs 14.1 and 14.3–6).

Fig 1.2 *A Victorian angel, in oak. Look how the flow of the drapery sweeps up to the knee and forms a cradle of space for the elbow – a beautiful design*

Fig 1.3 *Life-sized figures of the apostles designed and carved by Egid Asam in the Benedictine monastery church in Rohr, southern Germany*

MATERIAL

Obviously in our case this is wood: our ideas or visions are manifested out of dead trees (Fig 1.4). To a profound extent the material will lead the design. Different materials have different, and particular, properties, and must be handled and worked in appropriate ways. The result of carving hard wood with gouges (Fig 1.5) will (should) look distinctly different from that of modelling soft clay with the fingers; and the factors which make a design suitable for clay, to be fired or cast in bronze, will most often not be appropriate for wood.

TECHNIQUE

This is the mechanical skill of carving – the actual way the design is executed in the wood. It involves an understanding of the tools and how to sharpen and handle them, as well as the whole process whereby woodcarvings are made (Fig 1.6). Technique also includes intangible qualities such as perceptiveness or flair, which arise out of temperament, training and practice.

I now find that there is nothing new in analysing into these three elements – carvers have no prerogative here. The elements of design, materials and technique apply to all sculpture and to art in general, and certainly to all handcrafts.

It is extremely important to understand that *none of these three aspects is independent from another* – one must have the others in order to make sense. They are as interrelated and as indispensable as the three legs on a milking stool. Let us now look at them in more detail.

THE THREE ELEMENTS OF WOODCARVING

DESIGN

In other words, what you intend to carve. You need to think about your idea, about what additional information you will need. You must plan your approach and how you will use your wood.

Fig 1.4 *English oak. Every tree, and each part of a tree, is unique – as are carvers, their ideas, and the way they work*

Fig 1.6 *Disaster! Although the wood fibres were directed along the hind legs – the best possible option in this design – there was still a limit to the strength available. Returning to work on the head, gripping the base rather than the body, the fragile legs broke. Woodcarvers need to be constantly aware of such limitations*

IDEAS

It takes practice and experience to become a competent carver; after this, it is really the idea which separates one carver from another. *What* you carve is related to *why* you carve. It might be that you carve for money, and make what people want to commission or buy; or you may just love birds, or abstract forms, or old furniture. Where ideas come from is discussed in my previous book, *Relief Carving in Wood: A Practical Introduction* (page 127).

It is common for students to wait until they finish one carving before thinking about the next. I advise students to work on three carvings at a time: one starting (even if at the design stage), one in the middle stages, and one coming to its end. This way you never get stuck (see Sources of Inspiration on page 114).

PLANNING

Even the simplest carving requires a moment's thought beforehand. Right from the start you must be asking, at least:

Fig 1.5 *Detail of Fig 1.3. Although washed with paint, what you see is unmistakably the effects of carving: strong changes of plane and the direct impact of the tools*

- How will the design work in wood, taking account of wood's inherent strengths and weaknesses (Fig 1.7)?

- What material is available? Can glue lines be hidden, faults carved away? Is the colour or figure appropriate to the subject?

- What tools are available? These need to be to hand when you want them. Students often design something tiny (such as the eyes in a face), or deep, then find they have no small or bent tools to cope.

- Especially if the design is complicated, how will the work be held?

- What finish will you be giving the piece: tooled? sanded? a mixture?

- How suitable will this finish be to the subject (Fig 1.8)?

- If it is to be coloured, then do you know whether your choice of wood will take the colouring materials you want to use?

- How will the piece be mounted, or hung?

RESEARCH

All too many students start carving with the hope that it will all work out in the end. You cannot have too much information or do too much research, but you can have too little! 'Carving wood back on' to correct a mistake is quite an advanced technique, and in any case this is not always possible (see Mistakes and Repairs on page 104 for some alternative suggestions).

Another problem arises when a two-dimensional drawing is translated into a three-dimensional relief: suddenly parts of the subject are revealed that were not visible from the original viewpoint (see Drawing on page 34).

Your research may need to include making drawings, collecting a folder of illustrations or a 'morgue' of cuttings, finding a model, or making one in clay (see Modelling on pages 46–7).

Planning and research – knowing what you are doing and where you are going – give confidence. They are also an aid to freshness, and support spontaneity.

Fig 1.7 *This green man lives above my workshop door. The tool marks add vigour to the surface and the coarse oak gives just the right rough quality to the character*

Fig 1.8 *Stall end: monkey with berry and acanthus-leaf crocket; St Lorenz, Nürnberg, probably 15th century. The easy lines, and the way the design is calculated to add strength to the slender arms, are signs of a carver at home in his craft*

Fig 1.10 Joining up blocks for a large carving, in this case about 760mm (30in) high, requires great care and cannot be rushed

- The type of wood: will its structure and density take the detail you want? Is the wood carvable?

- Its strength, relative to the design: does the design need changing to accommodate it?

- Are weak elements supported?

- Can you use the grain to the best advantage, in both strength and appearance?

- Will the wood need to be joined? Are dowels appropriate? Joining is an element of 'technique', and it must be done well (Fig 1.10).

- Joined or not, is the piece seasoned? Will it move, or split? It is crucial to know both how to tell, and how to season (see my *Woodcarving Tools, Materials & Equipment*, pages 301–5).

- Defects in the wood may need to be repaired: what will be the best approach to this?

- How will you hold the wood? Do you need to leave waste areas for this purpose?

Fig 1.9 Sculpture in yew, 700mm (27in) high, by Mick Botten. The mountains and rivers of abstract carving require a profound understanding of the material

MATERIAL

Knowledge and understanding of your material does come with experience (Fig 1.9), but it's amazing how common sense is blown away by the winds of inspiration. Think about:

TECHNIQUE

There are four aspects to this element: the tools you need, the proper way to handle them, an understanding of carving methods, and a realistic assessment of your own ability.

TOOLS

I use, and teach the use of, traditional carving tools rather than burrs and cutters, rasps and sanding. The latter I differentiate (without a value judgement) more as wood 'shaping', but what I say here about regular carving tools would apply to any other carving or shaping techniques.

Carvers, with experience, develop an intimate understanding of their tools, learning what each of them can do and selecting them for their appropriateness for the job. The principle is a little like driving a car, which starts so self-consciously but eventually becomes automatic.

Carving tools must be sharpened correctly, the sharpness maintained and the tools properly cared for (Fig 1.11). The analogy in this case is with tuning a guitar before trying to play it – extremely important if you intend to play well! Sharpening is relatively straightforward; the problem is in getting students to accept this and not to see it as a chore, separate from carving (see Students' Problems on pages 122–3). Detailed information on tool selection and sharpening procedures is included in my earlier book *Woodcarving Tools, Materials & Equipment* (GMC Publications, 1994), and need not be repeated here.

So, you need to be considering:

- Do I have the right tools? If not, can I 'make do' or adapt?

- Do I have all the sharpening equipment to hand?

- Are the tools correctly sharpened?

- Can I keep them sharp?

HANDLING THE TOOLS

There are many ways of manipulating carving tools. The best allow the carver to be in control, work efficiently and achieve what is wanted with the least effort. The work then seems to progress more by intention than effort.

Different grips will be seen in the project photographs. See my *Relief Carving in Wood: A Practical Introduction* (page 24) for a full description of the two basic grips: 'low-angle' and 'pen and dagger'. Experience will also teach that the outcome of the tool – its effect on the wood – often depends as much on the way the blade is manipulated as on its sweep or profile.

THE CARVING PROCESS

In general, as the projects show, there are certain patterns – ways of approaching a lump of wood and transforming it into a version of your ideas – consistent enough to be termed the 'carving process' (see Notes on the Carving Process, page 24).

In this book I have, on the whole, kept to a simple distinction between roughing out, bosting in, modelling, detailing and finishing stages, and I mention other general carving principles in context. The ways carvers work are by no means fixed, so these are not 'rules'. However, they do resemble rules in that unwanted consequences may follow if they are disregarded by the inexperienced. An example would be carving details too soon, which will have to be removed and recarved at a later stage; or undercutting the edge of a leaf before finding out that it must be placed further back into the design.

When you get stuck, you can often revert to the logic of the process to help you out. All carvers have their own ways of working but, even if they don't realize it, the best of them aim for a performance that is disciplined and efficient – one which enables them to realize shapes and forms quickly, does not expose them to danger, and avoids having to undo work. With experience this process comes instinctively, from the heart (Fig 1.12).

ABILITY

I have yet to come across any student who has not had *some* ability, both in mechanical and artistic skills, to enable them to make some progress in woodcarving. It is also true that some are more 'gifted' than others: they are wired differently, and that's that. In the London Marathon, everyone is a winner who finishes. Woodcarving is like this – just doing it can bring its own reward, its own sense of personal success and achievement.

However, the effect of consistent and intelligent practice on any level of ability cannot be underestimated. Whatever degree of ability and resources we arrive with, much progress can be made with practice.

Woodcarving is never ending, it is in some sense always beginning. Practice means setting yourself

Fig 1.11 *Sharp tools are essential for the work, and a real pleasure to feel, hear and use in their own right*

Fig 1.12 *The head of the angel shown in Fig 1.2. Despite damage, the sense of a being within the wood is strong, and is an expression of the carver*

tasks and challenges, calling on resources, trying new approaches, making changes, gaining experiences, to improve on your skills. Woodcarving can be very hard work, yet also, as Gino Masero says on page 145, 'Carving is a sort of joy.'

HOW TO USE THIS BOOK

This chapter has described my particular approach to woodcarving, and provides thoughts to carry through the rest of the book. Between the various project chapters I have inserted considerations and advice on various topics which I want to emphasize. I hope that as a whole you can see how design, material and technique interrelate throughout the book. There is no particular order to the parts – ransack them as you will.

As this is a project book, you are welcome to follow and copy the projects. As with all project books – not just this one – please acknowledge the source of the carving if you are exhibiting or putting work into competition. Better still, use these projects as starting points for your own ideas, in which case, if your result looks very different to mine, no acknowledgement is necessary.

Many of the basics of woodcarving have been dealt with in greater depth in my earlier books, *Woodcarving Tools, Materials & Equipment, Lettercarving in Wood: A Practical Course* and *Relief Carving in Wood: A Practical Introduction*, which also contain some useful reference materials. Rather than sacrifice new material for old, I refer to these other books where appropriate.

CHAPTER TWO

HOLDING METHODS

SCREWS AND BENCHES

Ways of holding workpieces appear with every project in this book – they *must* do. Sometimes I change my method of holding the carving more than once, as its shape changes or access is needed to some particular area. I am striving to hold my work in the most favourable or advantageous way at all times. Over the years – and this will be true of all experienced carvers – I have eventually established a reliable repertoire of well-tried favourites.

Holding carving work is for many beginners something that just sort of 'happens'. More experience will tell them that it is actually an aspect of carving that needs careful consideration very early on, and something experienced carvers will give thought to in the initial planning stages.

Beginners to woodcarving spend, quite rightly, a lot of their time getting hold of carving tools and learning how to sharpen them. As they want to carve more, they find a place to do it regularly and make a bench on which to work. It is only as the variety of carving increases, with more complicated shapes and larger sizes, that they encounter more problems in holding the workpiece than can be handled by a couple of G-clamps (C-clamps) and the bench vice.

At this stage many newcomers look at the range and cost of holding devices available and decide they have spent enough already on tools, benchstones and so on, without having to spend yet more. The result is that their carving suffers: some carvings will not be undertaken; others will only be accomplished with yogic difficulty; yet others will end up poorly carved because the work couldn't be got at conveniently.

Woodcarving, when compared with many activities, both leisure and professional, is actually relatively inexpensive. The tools last for generations, the material can be free and economically used. It is also a fairly clean, creative occupation that can be done in all weathers! Compare it to woodturning or golf, for example.

Nevertheless, if you haven't the money to invest, you haven't; but, luckily, what many students do have is time. What I want to look at in this chapter is two particular ways in which work-holding possibilities can be increased enormously at little financial cost:

- The carver's screw: a versatile and inexpensive holding device, of which some students even make their own versions.

- Tilting or adjustable surfaces and benches: a range of work stations that can be made cheaply, and which combine well with the screw to help make working on carvings easier.

The factors making up an ideal holding device, as well as many options and suggestions for benches, were described in chapter 6 of *Woodcarving Tools, Materials & Equipment*. Here is a brief summary of the main points:

- Work must be immovable while carving, but able to be repositioned easily.

- There must be as much access as possible, if only to the area actually being carved.

- The holding device must not damage the carving.

- The carver must be able to work safely and comfortably.

Cost is often a factor, and must of course be balanced with benefits.

You will see that, while not suitable for everything, the carver's screw and the following ideas for work surfaces fulfil these criteria well, and will greatly facilitate your carving for only a little outlay. A cheap cousin to the screw, and a very useful device to go with the work surfaces described later, is the carver's clamp described on page 15.

WOODCARVERS' SCREWS

Carvers have been using such screws probably since the tapered thread was first invented. Woodcuts from southern Germany of around 1500 seem to show screws being used while large figures are being carved horizontally between the ends of collapsible frames (see *Woodcarving Tools, Materials & Equipment*, page 124). These frames, incorporating woodcarvers' screws, are still used today in southern Germany (Fig 2.1).

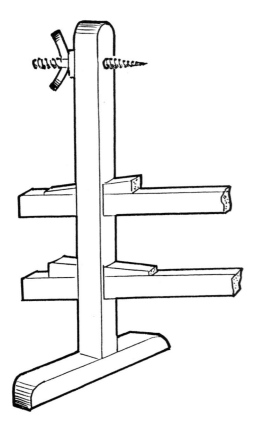

The woodcarver's screw is a device often overlooked or underrated today, especially by beginners, and seems hardly known in the USA. The screw and the carver's 'chops' (a kind of wooden vice) were often the only holding devices to be found in woodcarving shops not that long ago, and at roughly the cost of a G-clamp, I think the screw certainly deserves to find its way back again.

The advantage of the woodcarver's screw is that it holds the workpiece firmly, yet by slackening off the fly the wood can be rotated – a function to some extent taken over by the adjustable vices now available. It also hides away and keeps the work clear, unlike clamps, and the risk of damaging carving tools is nil – unless you carve into the screw. It is also relatively cheap.

I find myself using this holding method frequently, accompanied either by simple wooden supports or the tilting benches described in the next section. I find the carver's screw a flexible and handy way of holding work, directly or indirectly; its simplicity might even be said to be have an elegance about it. Used properly – that is, effectively – such screws can deal with a surprising range of situations. The carver's screw is certainly not without its limitations, but then, what device isn't?

DESCRIPTION

The carver's screw has three elements (Fig 2.2):

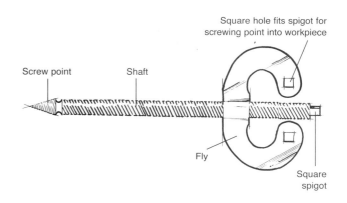

Fig 2.1 One end of an adjustable frame, similar to those shown in old woodcuts, still used today in southern Germany. (The other end is a mirror image of this one.) A carving is held between the two ends by carvers' screws driven into waste wood

Fig 2.2 The parts of a woodcarver's screw – in this case the graceful old Marples screw, no longer made but still to be found

1   The **point**: a tapered thread which screws into the workpiece, be it the back of a panel or the base of a three-dimensional carving.

2   The **shaft**: a bolt-like threaded bar which passes through a hole in whatever supports the carving, most typically a bench or other work surface.

3   The **fly**: a winged nut which draws the workpiece against the bench and fixes it in position. By loosening this fly, the work may be adjusted or revolved. In some models the fly may be replaced by a plastic knob or handle.

If the fly is large, there will be a square hole in one wing which fits a square spigot on the free end of the threaded bar; the fly can then be used as a spanner to tighten the screw into the carving (Fig 2.3). On models which have a knob instead, part of the shaft has to be faceted to take a separate spanner.

SOME EXAMPLES

A comparison between three readily available examples (Fig 2.4), varying in size and specification, will illustrate the strengths and weaknesses of these tools, how woodcarvers' screws actually work, and how to get the best out of them.

The screw by Axminster Power Tool Centre is made of steel in two sizes: 175mm (7in) long with a diameter of 12mm (½in), and a larger 230mm (9in) length with a diameter of 16mm (⅝in). Tightening the point into the wood is done by applying a spanner (not included) to the square spigot at the end of the shaft. A large, lobed plastic knob tightens the work to the work surface; the larger model also has a hole for a small tommy bar. The shaft is threaded along its whole length. The angle of the coarsely threaded point is 23° for the larger screw, and 17° for the smaller.

The Veritas is the shortest and lightest screw available, about 125mm (5in) long and made of brass. It has a hexagonal shank, for which a separate spanner is needed, which turns into 50mm (2in) of thread for the plastic clamping knob to run along. The angle of the deep and finely threaded point is only about 4° off parallel, and it comes to a 'sawn-off' end.

The Austrian Stubai woodcarvers' screws are made of steel and very businesslike. Two sizes are available. The larger is 275mm (11in) long with a diameter of 18mm (¾in), and has a large, purposeful fly some 200mm (8in) across, which is also used as a spanner to wind the screw into the wood by the hardened spigot, as seen in Fig 2.3. The smaller screw is 200mm (8in) long and 13mm (½in) in diameter. Stubai screws have a broad, open thread by comparison with the others (and conventional screws and coach screws), and do their work by compressing the wood fibres, rather than cutting into them. The larger screw has a point angle of 5°, and the smaller 7°.

Marples made the only available carver's screw in the UK for a very long time, but have now ceased producing it; there must, however, be many still around. It has a beautiful cast-iron fly, used as a spanner in the same manner as Stubai's screw, but

Fig 2.3 On some models, a square hole in the fly engages a spigot formed on the free end of the screw, enabling the fly to be used as a wrench to tighten the point into the workpiece

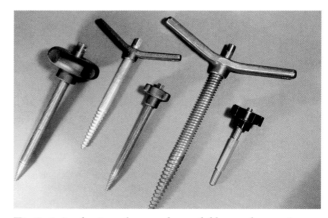

Fig 2.4 A selection of currently available woodcarvers' screws (left to right): large Axminster, small Stubai, small Axminster, large Stubai, Veritas

this suffers from being a poor fit on the soft, square end-spigot, and commonly rounds the spigot corners over. The screw has a point angle of 35°.

Several other firms make carvers' screws. It is essentially a simple tool, but there is more to it than meets the eye, and this is especially to be considered if you intend making one yourself. Coach (or lag) screws can be substituted for manufactured carvers' screws, but the specially designed screws are more sophisticated in their points and are generally easier to use.

How carvers' screws work

The principle is straightforward enough: the point of the carver's screw is fixed to the workpiece by boring a pilot hole in some hidden or waste part of the piece of wood to be carved, and then winding the point in, either with a spanner or with the spanner-like fly.

As with any screw fixing, the pilot hole takes up the unthreaded centre core of the screw, so that the winding serves only to screw the cutting threads into the surrounding wood. Indeed, without a pilot hole it may be impossible to drive a screw into hard wood at all. Once the point is in the workpiece, the shaft is inserted through a hole in the bench, and the fly or knob is used to tighten it in place.

There are useful points to be made by breaking this process down:

SCREWING INTO THE WORK
Grain direction

Depending on the carving, you may want to use the carver's screw either along (with) the grain (fixing, say, an upright figure from beneath), or across the grain (say, an animal on an integral base with the grain horizontal).

All woodworkers know that the best grip a woodscrew gets is when the thread grips *across* the wood fibres – the fibres are not cut, so much as caught between the metal threads (Fig 2.5). Threading *along* the fibres will tend to *cut* them: the wood can then tear away from the screw, which works loose easily and may even pull out. This is especially so if the fibres are soft or not densely packed, or if the work is large, or the leverage on the far end of the carving is great.

So, as a guide: of the two positions, fixing across the grain will give the firmest and most reliable grip and should be chosen where possible. (A tip here: if you screw the point into the wood tightly, then take it out and put a little wood glue on the point before reinserting it, this will bind the fibres together and help to stop them breaking up.)

The type of thread used on the Stubai screw works by *compressing* fibres, rather than cutting them, and so works well in both grain directions.

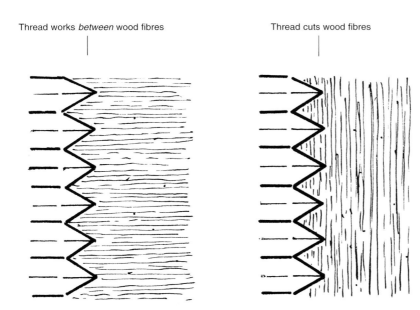

Thread works *between* wood fibres

Thread cuts wood fibres

Fig 2.5 *Screw threads cutting across (left) and along the grain. Note how the thread on the right will tend to cut off the fibres rather than slip between them; this makes it a much weaker way of fixing*

Point angle

The thread of the point cuts into the walls of the pilot hole as it is wound in, and this is what makes the carver's screw grip. It stands to reason that a screw which has only a slight taper at its point will come closer to gripping the walls of the pilot hole – with less tendency to pull out – than one with a wide-angled point (Figs 2.6–2.8).

The available screws that are only slightly tapered (such as the Veritas and Stubai) have more impressive holding powers than wider-angle ones. It may be that a wider angle will have all the holding power you want for the work you do, but it is usually better to have more available as your work develops. An angle of around 20° is about the maximum that is really useful – the less the better – and you should avoid anything larger. The old Marples screw with an angle of 35° has a poor grip and is limited in what it can hold, especially with the grain.

FITTING TO THE BENCH OR WORK SURFACE

Once the carver's screw has been tightened into the carving, the parallel shaft is inserted through a hole in the bench. The fly or knob is then tightened beneath. The carving is now firmly gripped to the bench top, ready for work.

To those unused to them, the shafts of the longer screws often seem inordinately overlong. With a bench, say, 50mm (2in) thick, the knob or fly has to be run down a long way before it tightens underneath the bench. However, this extra length widens the options of how these tools may be used.

The shortest of the screws considered here (Veritas) has only a 50mm (2in) hexagonal shaft (for the spanner) for passing through the bench – so for the average bench there is no problem with slack. There would be the opposite problem if working on a thicker surface, or from a carving post, for example. The Axminster and Stubai screws – especially the larger versions – are considerably longer, with a lot more shaft passing through our average bench to be taken up by the fly.

When the carving is fixed to the bench top for work, this invariably means taking up the slack under the bench with a wooden washer – either

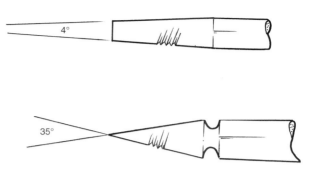

Fig 2.6 The points of carvers' screws have significantly different tapers, with consequently differing gripping properties

Fig 2.7 Three points close up, showing a range of angles which manufacturers think suitable. On the left is the old Marples, with an extreme angle of about 35°

Fig 2.8 This cross section neatly compares the amount of grip possible in the workpiece by screws with different point angles: the Veritas screw (left) and the Marples

because (with the Veritas) some of the hexagonal bar protrudes, or because running the fly back up such a length for tightening is a little tedious. However, you *can* use this extra length – and reduce the amount of tightening needed – in two ways:

- By boring a clearance hole and 'losing' some of the shaft inside the carving; this allows the point to grip well up inside the workpiece, giving a firmer support against the leverage of carving and making the grip of the thread more secure.

- By standing the workpiece higher off the bench, on a block or packing piece, and so raising it to a higher working height (Figs 2.9 and 2.10). This is certainly an advantage at times: if the carving sits directly on the bench, not only will the bench surface get cut, but the lowest parts of the carving may be awkward to get at.

Fig 2.9 Holding work directly on the bench may make access around the base difficult. A wooden-block 'washer' beneath the bench takes up some of the screw shaft

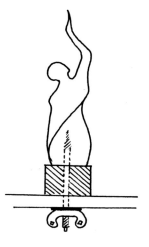

Fig 2.10 Placing a block beneath the carving gains extra work height as well as taking up some of the length of the screw

A longer screw also allows you to work on a thicker surface, such as a post (see next page), and get at areas that are otherwise difficult.

These are all advantages for the longer carvers' screws, but again it may be that a shorter one is all you need for your particular work.

SOME OTHER ASPECTS OF WORKING WITH CARVERS' SCREWS

PLACING THE POINT

I said earlier that the screw must be strategically positioned in a waste or unimportant part of the wood. The place chosen must of course be thick and strong enough, and definitely in wood that is not needed for carving. But sometimes you may not know exactly what your carving will look like; you may be making it up as you go along, and you may want to be able to change things. In this case, glue on a piece of waste wood and screw into that, removing the waste later. Hot-melt glue works well for this purpose.

Make your hole only as deep as you need to get a grip. A common fault is misjudging the depth and then meeting the hole by carving from the other direction (Fig 2.11).

Fig 2.11 The pilot hole for the screw from the back has met the carving from the front. Luckily this will probably be unobtrusive if repaired with a Dutchman (see pages 65–6) and overcarved

HOLES

A drawback of the carver's screw is the need to bore into the carving: this, obviously, leaves a hole behind. Normally this is simply plugged with a slightly tapered cylinder in matching wood, glued in and neatly trimmed off. As the hole is behind or beneath the carving it is of no consequence.

If you absolutely *must not* have a hole, then glue on waste wood first, as suggested above. With paper glued between waste and carving, you can split the waste off easily when finished.

HOLDING BOARDS

Not everyone wants to have holes in their beautiful bench; I tend to think more functionally, and have as many as are useful. One way to avoid them is to have a thick board clamped to the bench top which overhangs sufficiently to allow the fly to be turned underneath. This actually can give you far better access to the carving than when it is on the bench itself, and is my preferred method (see Fig 11.14 on page 121).

Fixing the carving to your bench is only one way of using the carver's screw. As implied earlier, you can insert the screw through a block held in the bench vice, which is particularly good if you object to holes in the bench. If this 'block' is actually a vertical board or post, then you have a whole new set of positions to carve in. Over the years I have accumulated a variety of posts and pieces of wood with holes for carvers' screws, which live under the bench, ready for fixing carvings to. As will be seen shortly, carvers' screws also operate well when combined with an adjustable work surface.

ADJUSTMENT ALONG A WORK SURFACE

Instead of using a fixed hole, or even a series of them, my tilting work surfaces have the carver's screw pass through a *slot*: the work can be slid along, up or down.

Tilting the work surface backwards or forwards, sliding the carving along the slot, and rotating it means there is a lot of freedom for repositioning a carving. Do experiment with different posts, boards and surfaces, and you will find their versatility considerably greater than you might expect.

WASHERS

Rather than wait until you need them, prepare a selection of wooden blocks or washers at different thicknesses for use under the carving or behind the bench; and keep them to hand.

None of these carvers' screws come with a metal washer, but one is strongly advisable to stop the fly chewing into the supporting wood or bench.

PILOT HOLES

Make sure you bore the starting hole perpendicular to a flat face in order to get the best frictional grip on the bench. You may like to countersink the hole slightly to allow room for the wood bulging as the screw enters.

PREVENTING THE WORK ROTATING

Sometimes during heavy carving, particularly with blows from a mallet, the moment about the screw fixing causes the work to turn. Increase the friction between the carving and the bench with offcuts of thin rubber or sleeping mat, leather, cork tiles, or two sheets of fine sandpaper glued back to back.

I may even use two screws when heavy roughing out is needed, sacrificing the ability to rotate the work for the time being.

CORROSION

Bear in mind the corrosive qualities of some woods – classically damp oak – on iron if you leave a steel screw in a long time. In such cases, treat the screw end with an iron phosphate rust inhibitor as used on car bodywork, or take it out between carving sessions. Always brush the screw threads clean before storing.

The Veritas brass carver's screw is corrosion-proof; but you must have an exactly fitting steel spanner (Fig 2.12) if you are not to damage the softer metal.

Fig 2.12 The Veritas screw needs a well-fitting spanner to impel it into the workpiece

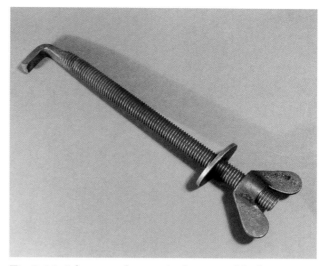

Fig 2.13 A home-made carver's clamp, useful when combined with tilting surfaces

BUYING YOUR CARVER'S SCREW

The Stubai type of screw is comparatively expensive, but its ability to grip by compression into both end and side grain, in addition to its overall size, makes it the choice for larger carvings. With the other screws you need to look at the size and the point angle in particular, and whether you are happy with the method of tightening – some students, for example, find the hard plastic knobs painful or difficult to use.

Carvers' screws do have their limitations, but given their usefulness they all represent a cheap, valuable addition to any carver's kit. Indeed, such screws may well be the only holding devices some carvers ever need.

THE WOODCARVER'S CLAMP

Instead of ending in a threaded point, the carver's clamp ends in a 'dog' or flat face bent at right angles to the shaft (Fig 2.13). This device works like a bench holdfast and can grip work like an ordinary clamp, but with far less metal in the way. They are not available to buy but are straightforward to make with heat and a hammer.

The carver's screw can be turned into a clamp or holdfast by screwing it into a suitable block of wood to form an overall T-shape.

THREE CARVING STANDS

I designed and made these three stands to make the best use of the woodcarver's screw, although they are generally useful for supporting carvings in other ways as well.

You will see the very successful tilting work surfaces being used in many projects in this book: the lighter, simpler tilting surface or 'deckchair stand' for smaller reliefs, and the free-standing tilting bench for larger pieces. The adjustable carving platform has only recently joined the team, and has already proved its worth for three-dimensional carvings.

I made up the three carving stands with what materials I had to hand, and I expect readers will adapt and make their own versions in the same way. So I will not be giving exact plans – only the principles, some working notes, a few measurements and some illustrations.

VERTICAL CARVING

A large proportion of my relief carving is done with the work vertical, or nearly vertical, and I encourage students to do the same. What are the pros and cons of working in this way?

ADVANTAGES

- You can stand back to look at the whole work, rather like an artist at the easel; this is particularly suitable for larger relief carvings.

- The carving is orientated as it will be when finished, and can be lit accordingly.

- There is no distorting of perspective.

- You can get at every part of the carving easily, without over-reaching.

- Wood chips and shavings readily fall away.

DISADVANTAGES

- Carving tools must be placed on a side table (mine has castors and moves around with me) – but this only means a new working habit. An alternative would be a hinged flap on either side of the stand.

- Less body weight can be put behind a cut when standing to a vertical carving than when leaning over one placed horizontally.

THE BALANCE

In my experience the disadvantages are far outweighed by the benefits. If you have never carved in this way, I strongly suggest you try it. It does not mean that you won't need a horizontal surface, particularly for work in the round. The tilting bench can be returned to horizontal when required, and even with three-dimensional work on an adjustable swivel-ball clamp, it can still be an advantage to use the tilt facility.

A NOTE ON MATERIALS

I made all three carving stands from hardwood offcuts, salvaged board ends, old fence posts, etc., so the timber cost was very low. I used predominantly oak – this is what I had – but beech, ash, sycamore, mahogany, etc. would do equally well. Softwood has less weight and more spring – not such a good option, since the more solid a carving support can be, the better.

A few items of metalwork, such as bolts or hinges, are needed. These are easy and inexpensive to buy, and are often to be found in the corners of most workshops. The exception is the pair of metal arc braces for the tilting bench; these I had specially made. Shop around: small engineering firms have different facilities and costs.

TILTING BENCH

I described the original idea for a tilting worksurface, as used by the late Gino Masero, in my *Woodcarving Tools, Materials & Equipment* (page 260). Since then I have played with the bench design and it is a modified – and, I think, improved – version of the original that I describe here (Figs 2.14–2.16).

The metal arc braces allow the work surface to tilt back incrementally from the vertical. Relief or other carvings can be raised, lowered or rotated by means of the central slot. The bench also doubles as a normal horizontal carving bench to which vices and other holding devices can be attached.

Fig 2.14 A full view of the bench with the tilting work surface in a near-vertical position, supported by arc-shaped metal braces. The central slot in the work surface takes a woodcarver's screw, as do the holes to the side when I wish to work nearer the edge. The two fittings in the upper corners are to take an adjustable lamp, which can be seen in several of the photographs in Chapter 8

Fig 2.15 The bench tilted at 45°; the metal arcs slide down within the bench framework

Fig 2.16 The tilting surface lowered and locked in a horizontal position. Note how the upper cross rail at the front is set well below the top, so that there is full access underneath to the fly of the carver's screw

CONSTRUCTION

Consider the top (the work surface) as separate from the supporting frame beneath.

WORK SURFACE

The working surface is 900mm (36in) by 600mm (24in), and 50mm (2in) thick. It is made from two boards of wood braced together at each end, leaving a slot between them along which the carver's screw can slide. This slot allows more flexible and easier positioning of the relief carving than a series of holes – although I also have several holes bored into the surface, and add more as I find I need them. It is vital that the strength lost by having a slot is regained in the joinery.

Allow at least 50mm (2in) between the work surface and the supporting rail beneath it: you need to leave this gap at each side so that you can still get at the locking wing nuts when the top is in the horizontal position. (This can be seen most clearly in Fig 2.16.)

HEIGHT

The height of the work surface must be established to suit your own height: in the horizontal position, it should be a little below your elbow level as you stand. In my case the bench is about 1m (40in) high with the top lowered.

FRAME

The frame legs are 100 x 100mm (4 x 4in) in section. All the base-frame joints are mortised and tenoned, and pinned. The deep base rails form a box (Fig 2.17) for storing heavy workshop objects, which increases the stability of the bench when the work surface is raised.

In order that the fly of the carver's screw can be easily got at and adjusted, I lowered the upper cross rails at each end. This makes the base frame something of an H-shape when looked at from the end (Fig 2.18).

The upper cross rails on each side are capped with a flat board to take the locking plates.

Fig 2.17 *A floor is fitted between the bottom rails, making a box in which heavy objects can be placed for additional stability*

Fig 2.19 *A flange or bracket fixes the arc supports to the back of the work surface.*

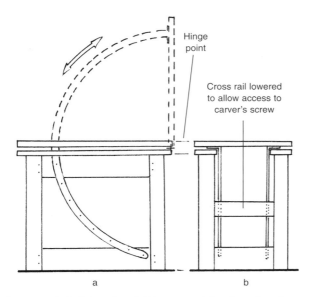

Fig 2.18 *Side (a) and end (b) views of the tilting bench (not to scale)*

METAL FITTINGS

There are three items of metalwork to consider: the arc supports, the hinges and the locking plates.

Arc supports

A pair of metal arcs, *as closely matched as possible*, braces the work surface. These are the heart of the bench: start here if you are designing the bench to a different specification. These braces can be exactly positioned once the top has been hinged to the base frame. (The locking brackets are sited last.)

I took an accurate full-size plywood template of the arcs to a local engineering firm, who cut them from 10mm (⅜in) steel, bored matching 10mm holes to take the locking pins, and welded on the flange by which the arcs are bolted to the back of the work surface (Fig 2.19).

(The design shown in *Woodcarving Tools, Materials & Equipment* has the arcs fixed to the *edge* of the work top – hence the three holes in Fig 2.19, which are now redundant – but more solid support comes from bracing directly on the back.)

The brackets are true arcs, somewhat longer than quarter-circles, and have a radius centred at the hinges on which the bench top pivots (Fig 2.20). It is the radius from the hinge point to the centres of the locking holes which is the important measurement; on my bench this is 600mm (24in).

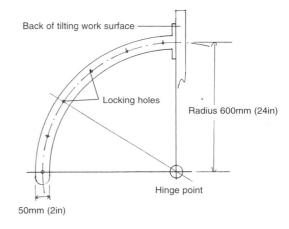

Fig 2.20 *The metal arc brackets (not drawn to scale) form the heart of the bench. To work efficiently they must be as true arcs of a circle as possible*

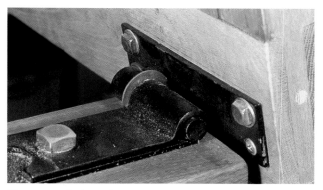

Fig 2.21 *The hinge between underframe and top: the washer takes up slack. The pivot (pin centre) of the hinge is the point from which the radius of the metal arc supports is measured*

Hinges

The hinges (Fig 2.21) are those used for farm gates, and have a strong pin from which the strap part of the hinge can be removed. They were overlong, and I used the offcuts to make the locking plates.

I chose these hinges for their strength: this is a tough bench and takes heavy work. They naturally create the gap mentioned earlier between the top and the frame beneath, but, as they tend to be crudely made, you may need to take up play around the pin with shim (such as metal from a tin can). Align the hinges with both pins pointing outwards.

Locking plates

The locking plates (Fig 2.22) are bent to shape from hinge offcuts and fixed to the underframe with studding and wing nuts. I preferred to provide a positive locking here, with removable wing nuts rather than, say, barrel bolts.

Slight differences in radius along the arcs (despite their being well made), coupled with small discrepancies in the woodwork, made it difficult to align the precisely sized holes in the arc with those in the locking plate. I overcame this by enlarging the hole in the plate where the bolt passes through to the underframe, and used a large washer under the wing nut to cover this (Fig 2.23). When this wing nut is slackened, the increased range of movement in the locking plate allows the holes of plate and arc to be aligned easily.

When the bench is finished you should find that, when locked in either vertical or horizontal position, there is no movement in the top.

Fig 2.22 *The locking plate or bracket is fixed by means of a length of studding which passes into the upper rail to a hole (seen in shadow behind the lower part of the arc) which takes the nut (see also Fig 2.23). The arc support is locked to the plate with a coach bolt and a second wing nut*

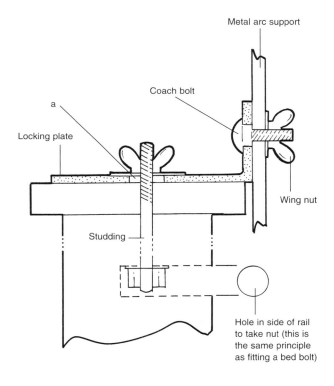

Fig 2.23 *The hole (a) in the locking plate, beneath the wing nut and its wide washer, is oversized to allow the plate to move around and adjust to any discrepancies in the holes or woodwork*

'DECKCHAIR' STAND

It was while actually gazing at a deckchair on a beach that I first had the idea for this carving stand (Fig 2.24), hence its name. The deckchair principle is easy to see.

Fig 2.24 The 'deckchair' adjustable stand for carving small reliefs. A Veritas carving screw fitted through the slot in the work surface allows the work to be raised, lowered or turned

This lightweight stand is popular among students. It can be easily transported to carving classes, but is surprisingly robust. It provides a work surface for small relief carvings, adjustable between vertical and 45°, and sits on a normal carving bench.

Again, because I normally use this stand with a carver's screw, it has a central slot. For this lightweight stand, I find the Veritas screw ideal. The workpiece can also be fixed with small clamps at the edge, or with wedges and fences tacked to the surface (see *Woodcarving Tools, Materials & Equipment*, pages 269–70).

CONSTRUCTION

The version shown was cobbled out of spare material, a minimum of 25mm (1in) thick; the work surface is made from blockboard. Measurements are given in Fig 2.25.

I made the slots in the rack by boring appropriate-sized holes and cutting out the waste with a jigsaw. If you start with thicker wood, you could split it to make a matching pair of racks. The

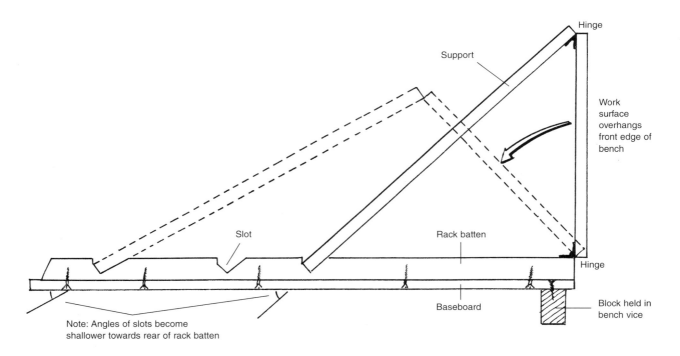

Hinge

Support

Work surface overhangs front edge of bench

Slot

Rack batten

Hinge

Baseboard

Block held in bench vice

Note: Angles of slots become shallower towards rear of rack batten

Overall height: 450mm (18in)
Width: 250mm (10in)
Length of rack batten: 700mm (28in)

Fig 2.25 Deckchair stand: principles and dimensions. This method of slotting the rack is an alternative to that shown in the photographs

bar joining the two back braces (Fig 2.26) was turned slightly larger than the starting holes in the rack: this means that the bar actually jams in the bottom of the slot and locks. The braces on each side should ideally touch the base at their ends to provide sideways stability.

A block at the front edge of the baseboard is gripped in the bench vice. With or without this, the deckchair stand can be clamped or bolted to the bench top.

As the hinges take a lot of strain – especially sideways – they must be as heavy-duty as possible.

Fig 2.26 View from above and behind the deckchair stand, showing the rack which allows the braces for the work surface to step backwards

ALTERNATIVES

The method of racking shown in the photographs is the one I first devised, but is now only one of several options which students have come up with:

- Use another piece of blockboard instead of two supporting arms, and simply round over the end to fit in the slots.

- Use blockboard again for the braces, keeping the ends square, and cutting the slots square at an appropriate angle (this alternative is shown in Fig 2.25).

- Use battens with angled faces on the baseboard, instead of a rack.

CARVING PLATFORM

Versions of this carving stand (Figs 2.27–2.29) have been used in south German and Austrian workshops for generations.

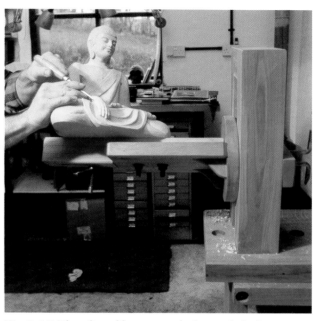

Fig 2.27 The adjustable carving platform is bolted or clamped to a bench surface. It raises, lowers or tilts the work. Holes in the work table can be used for carvers' screws, which also allow the carving to be rotated

Fig 2.28 Three-quarter front view of the adjustable platform

21

Fig 2.29 Side view. The brackets are housed into the disc and platform, and might be unnecessary if thicker wood were used

Adjustable holding devices in metal are increasingly common, and have tremendous advantages over fixed methods. However, this particular stand has a definite benefit not to be found in any adjustable vice on the market: the carving platform, or table, raises and lowers the workpiece *while it remains in its vertical position.*

If you are holding a tall carving in one of the commercial swivel-ball carving clamps, you may need to tilt the work, even to the horizontal, to get access to both the top and bottom of it. Sometimes the radical change of view that this causes is undesirable, and you would prefer simply to lift the carving higher – as you can, very simply, with this carving platform. You can also rotate the table through 360° if you need to, and rotate the workpiece itself (if you are using a carver's screw), so there is good access to the carving all round.

Other benefits for me are the pleasure to be had from working with a wooden device rather than a metal one, and the joy of making this elegant stand for practically nothing, using up offcuts and odd scraps of wood, and finding it does its job really well.

CONSTRUCTION

There are two parts to this carving platform: the stand, and the platform or table arrangement itself.

STAND

The stand has a base 50mm (2in) thick. I bolt it to the centre slot of my adjustable bench, described above, but it can be clamped instead.

The base measures 400 x 330mm (16 x 13in), with the uprights set towards one end. The table overhangs the larger portion.

The uprights are a substantial 75 x 100mm (3 x 4in) and are through-mortised, with a shouldered and wedged tenon, into the base. This construction is immensely strong, with no flexibility.

The height of the uprights will depend on how much 'lift' you want, bearing in mind that the disc will touch the base on its lowest setting. In my case the table moves through 300mm (12in), but one could conceivably make a much larger, floor-standing model.

PLATFORM

The platform assembly (Figs 2.30 and 2.31) consists of a carving table joined to a disc, which grips the front of the uprights in whichever position the table is rotated; a cylindrical 'washer' of wood glued to the back of the disc; and a backplate gripping the back of the uprights. The whole is clamped to the uprights with a central studding bar and large nut, wing nut or fly.

The construction is shown in Fig 2.32. The originals of these carving stands that I saw had a large woodcarver's screw instead of the studding – perfect, but a luxury I wasn't prepared to afford!

The table is 250 x 280mm (10 x 11in) and 45mm (1¾in) thick, mortised into the disc with wedged tenons. The disc is 230mm (9in) in diameter and similarly thick. The originals had a thicker table and disc, doing away with the small strengthening brackets (seen in Fig 2.29) which I felt were needed at this size.

The length of 18mm (¾in) studding passes along the axis of the table to a nut housed into the wood, as with a bed bolt. I found the easiest way was to glue up the table in pieces. I bored a centre piece for the studding, let in the nut from the side (that is, from *within* the table), filled any remaining space around the nut with a mixture of glue and wood dust, then glued and dowelled on the side pieces of the table. The large wooden 'washer', glued to the back of the disc and reinforced with a nut, should fit neatly between the uprights of the stand, with only a little play. It serves to keep the table in position as it is rotated.

Fig 2.30 *The platform assembly removed from the uprights*

CONCLUSION

For me, part of the joy of carving is the continual joy of innovation. These carving stands are only a few of many possibilities, but demonstrate how very useful aids can be made with little cost – mainly an investment of time – particularly when coupled with the inexpensive but very useful carving screw.

Woodcarvers need to pay attention to their work stations – the way they hold and work on carvings – but don't get hung up on getting 'everything just right' before you start carving, or else you will never start.

Fig 2.31 *Back view of the complete apparatus, showing the table assembly locked in position. The wooden 'washer', clearly visible behind the vertical disc, keeps the table aligned during adjustment*

Fig 2.32 *Details of the table assembly for the carving platform*

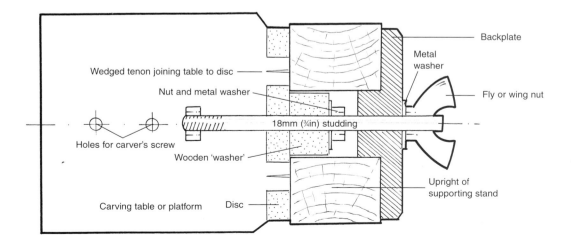

Wedged tenon joining table to disc

Nut and metal washer

Holes for carver's screw

Wooden 'washer'

Carving table or platform   Disc

18mm (¾in) studding

Backplate

Metal washer

Fly or wing nut

Upright of supporting stand

NOTES ON THE CARVING PROCESS

CENTAURS AND LIFELINES

Arriving at point B: your finished carving, having started at point A: an idea or desire, involves a path that I call 'the carving process'. It entails establishing, developing, balancing and finally fusing the three elements of design, material and technique in whatever way is uniquely appropriate to the particular work.

In the course of this book you will see this carving process broken down and described in progressive stages. Here I want to extract a few thoughts to ponder on:

PREPARATION

- **Information**: Research – which may include drawing and modelling where necessary – is crucial.

- **Practice**: You will not be able to carve the face you want if you have only been carving for a day; or if you have only ever, say, chip-carved; or if you have little time; or will only ever carve the one and move on – any more than you can expect a piano sonata to sound well under equivalent circumstances.

- **Planning**: Like a centaur, you can apply rational thought from above ('What should I do next?') or a more unconscious dynamism from below ('Just do it!'). You need to decide which is appropriate, but remember: problems usually arise through lack of foresight.

- Prepare base and back early; they are often difficult to work on later.

CARVING

- Carve the main masses or forms of the carving first (the 'bosting' or sketching stage). Subdivide these main masses into secondary ones, according to what you want to achieve, and consolidate and subdivide further until the final details just fall into place. This is essentially what is happening in each of the projects in this book as I proceed from 'roughing out' to 'bosting in' to 'modelling' to 'detailing' – although carving is not always as neat as this.

- The carving should look 'unfocused' to begin with, as the main masses and planes begin to appear, then increasingly 'focused' with subsequent modelling and detailing.

- Don't panic in the unfocused stages – carvings *will* look unprepossessing and unlike very much at all at this point; this is normal. You are (or should be) in control, even if it's hard to tell.

- The early stages are the most important. Don't be tempted to detail or fix exact positions too soon.

- **Lifelines**: Like climbers or potholers, throw lots of these as you go along. Mark high points first; take time to visualize; calculate and measure from your reference material; draw lines, write notes on the wood. If you are unsure, make a model, or a trial carving of the part.

- The carving is best worked *as a whole*: this means not finishing off one area while leaving another at a much rougher and earlier stage. All parts of a carving are relative: they work together with the other parts to create the total.

King's head in oak. The process from idea to finished carving can be long, mentally and emotionally taxing, and physically hard. Confidence and competence come with intelligent practice

CHAPTER THREE

HANDS

BY ALBRECHT DÜRER

Fig 3.1 *The finished carving in English oak*

Fig 3.2 *Hands by Albrecht Dürer (1471–1528)*

I must admit right at the start that I was in more than two minds about undertaking this small carving (Fig 3.1). I have had several requests over the years to convert famous paintings and drawings into carvings, and have always declined them. To begin with, I'm usually in awe of the original and, finding it satisfying enough, can't understand why anyone would want anything else. Then there is the matter of copying a work created in brush strokes or shaded lines (in reality two-dimensional with one viewpoint) into three-dimensional carving using an entirely different approach. Being now so far from the well-loved original, there is every chance of producing something that disappoints. And in this particular case, Albrecht Dürer's drawing of a pair of supplicating hands (Fig 3.2) is so well known as to be almost a cliché. I admit to inwardly groaning when I heard the request.

However, I made a big mistake before I declined the job: I let the persuasive smile of the mother superior from the Convent of Poor Clare into the house.

The Poor Clare nuns felt it appropriate to give a small copy of Albrecht Dürer's drawing, as a carving, to the architect who had overseen their move to Hereford and worked on the convent – a token of gratitude for his work.

Albrecht Dürer (1471–1528) – a contemporary of the great woodcarver Riemenschneider (see Chapter 14) – was one of the leading movers of the Gothic Renaissance, and his graphic work in the form of copper engravings and woodcuts had a great influence on European art. When I started to look closely at Dürer's drawing of the hands of a praying apostle – a study for an altarpiece commissioned in 1507 – I became absorbed in the very sculptural nature of the study: full of depth and sensitive detail, and with such a lovely sense of light. It is a small masterpiece, whether or not it seems somewhat jaded today as a result of over-exposure.

So who was I even to think of attempting a translation of this drawing into wood? I doubted I could catch anything like the feeling in these hands, so I opened my mouth to decline. Then the mother superior smiled beatifically at me – and of course I said I'd have a go...

DESIGN

I had a copy of the original study and I could see that its three-dimensional style was not unlike a fine preliminary sketch for carving or modelling anyway, so there was more sense in the attempt than I had first thought. Here, then, is a simple relief carving – the simplest project in this book, and the one which gives the clearest exposition of the basic approach to this sort of work.

One thing I did notice was that the hands were extraordinarily long, especially in the middle phalanxes of the fingers; I wanted to keep this sense of length. It was also not too clear where the heel of the right hand arose from, where the wrist becomes the forearm. The drawing is very three-dimensional and I felt I would need to make full use of the relief depth available to me.

What is important to remember is that *any drawing has only one viewpoint* and is actually in only one plane (see Drawing on page 34). A relief carving, on the other hand, has many viewpoints in addition to the main one, and physical depth to play with – in other words, one can really look around drawn corners.

Only simple outlines are needed to work from, none of the detail. I used a light box to get these preliminary outlines from the drawing, and then used a photocopier to arrive at my finished working size (Fig 3.3). You can use this drawing if you want to follow this carving, enlarging in the same way. I would suggest not making the hands any smaller than the 150mm (6in) I worked to, which is about two-thirds the size of the original.

When determining the size of the drawing, I allowed for a boundary line and a space to put the artist's initials in the corner – Dürer's monogram is as well known as his drawings, and although it does not appear in the original of this particular drawing, I felt this was an appropriate way to acknowledge where the carving originated.

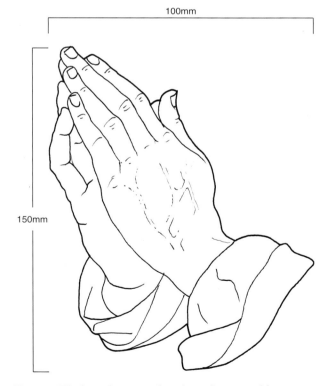

Fig 3.3 *Working drawing taken from the original by tracing with a light box*

WOOD

I used some English oak, 200mm (8in) along the grain (which ran vertically on the drawing), 145mm (5¾in)wide. With a total depth of 33mm (1⁵⁄₁₆in), I allowed 23mm (¹⁵⁄₁₆in) for the carving and left a background 10mm (⅜in) thick.

Oak has a rough strength which contrasts with – acts as a foil to – the refined surface of the flesh. It also has medieval, 'old-rugged-cross' connotations (even though limewood was used extensively for carving in Dürer's time). The detail in this carving is simple, which is the best option for open-grained oak. Many other woods might have been chosen – walnut, lime, mahogany – each of which would give a different 'feel' to the finished carving.

The wood needs to be accurately prepared all round, and the depth of the ground scored in with a marking gauge. Scoring like this gives a crisp and neat edge to work to.

The quickest way of laying out the carving is with carbon paper and a hard pencil or ball-point pen (Fig 3.4). Keep the working drawing by you for reference, but more importantly the original drawing, which you need to look at frequently.

HOLDING

I attached the work with double-sided carpet tape to a piece of clean plywood, which in turn was fixed to the carving bench with clamp and holdfast. You might prefer to use a vertical stand instead, but I found that the small size of this carving allowed me to work easily around it without perspective distortion.

CARVING

GROUNDING OUT

The first stage of most relief carving is usually to remove and clean up the background (or more simply the 'ground') as quickly as possible: this is termed **grounding out**.

I used a bench drill for preliminary waste removal (Fig 3.5), coming in close to my drawn outline. A router would also do this job efficiently. Without such mechanical help, you would need to start straight away with the deep gouge and mallet as described below.

Fig 3.4 *Transferring the working drawing to the wood with carbon paper*

Fig 3.5 *Boring away the background waste with the bench or pillar drill*

BENCH DRILL

Several points concerning the use of the bench drill are worth noting:

- Most importantly, make sure everything – chuck, depth stop, etc. – is *locked tightly before you start*. You can bore to quite fine tolerances, but the last thing you want is for the bit to sink deeper into the wood without your noticing it.

- Enough wood must be left above the final ground level for finishing with carving tools, bearing in mind that most drill bits, including the Forstner bit that I used, have a projecting point – it is this point which determines the depth to which you must work (Fig 3.6).

- If you change bit sizes to get in closer to the outline, check that the bits are not different lengths. If they are, you will need to adjust the depth stop or the table height

- For the bit to run true, the centre point must have guiding wood in which to bite; so don't overlap holes too much, or the wood may crumble and the bit wander. Take especial care near the edge, where the bit cannot cut a full circle.

Fig 3.6 How to allow for the point of the drill bit when boring waste

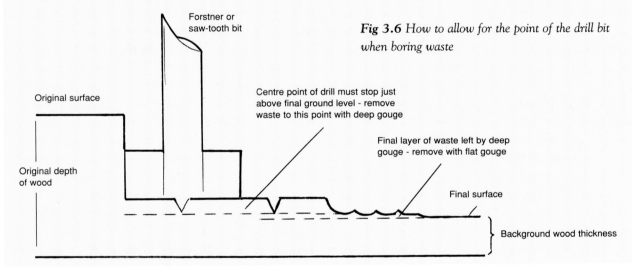

Fig 3.7 shows the wasted ground and the marks left by the drill, with the subsequent stage of carving under way. A deep gouge (about no. 8) is worked methodically across the ground, with a mallet, using the marks made by the point of the drill as a depth guide, and gently approaching the walls of the carving proper. Again a small depth of waste is left for the next stage, which is levelling the ground.

There is no need to make the ground 'engineering' flat – it must just look and feel flat. Using a flat gouge (no. 3, or Swiss no. 2), trim off the ridges left by the deep gouge, paring the surface cleanly to the finished depth marked by the gauge line. If you have been careful and accurate with the deep gouge, the final clean and level surface, with a faintly faceted effect, appears very quickly (Fig 3.8).

Fig 3.7 Removing waste to slightly above the final depth with a deep gouge

Fig 3.8 Finishing the ground with a flat gouge by paring away the ridges left by the deep gouge

SETTING IN

Next, trim back the waste wood to the outline of the hands with carving tools of appropriate curvature – this is known as **setting in** the subject (Fig 3.9).

The (vertical) walls of the outline and the background must be brought together neatly. As the work is eventually to be undercut, it is important *not to cut below the final ground level* at this time – better to leave the corners between walls and ground with a little amount of waste in them. Try to be as accurate as possible, but don't follow the outline slavishly, as there needs to be some room for adjustment as you go along.

Fig 3.9 Setting in the outline. You can see that a little leeway has been allowed here – when the shaping of the hands has progressed further, the outline can be trued up by eye

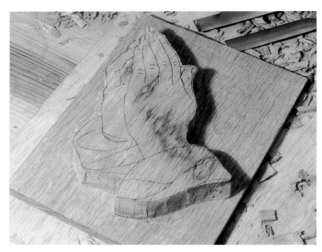

Fig 3.10 The ground is finished, the hands set in and ready for shaping

This is a typical way of grounding out and setting in a relief subject, ready for the following stages of carving proper. At this point the hands look cut out and stuck on to the background (Fig 3.10).

BOSTING IN

The first step is to find the main **planes** of the hands – that is, the directions and positions of the main surfaces – and separate the main masses. This rough 'sketching' gives the overall plan of the piece, and it is worth pausing at this point to consider coldly what your best approach is. It is here that studying Dürer's original drawing is crucial. Think in terms of big shapes, not details. For example, decide where the high points need to be: in this case the upper little finger and the tip of the lower little finger where they touch; also the centre of the upper cuff. Visualize how the wood will 'flow away' from these points. There is bound to be *some* leeway: an acknowledgement that this carving can only ever be an interpretation.

In Fig 3.11 the upper (left) hand has been sloped right back to just above the ground so as to make full use of the available depth and establish the overall shape. This is done before the fingers and thumb are separated. The right hand has been lowered, except at the fingertips. Both sleeves are knocked into rough shape and the wrists cut into them.

At the end of this stage there should be a fairly clear sense of the form emerging.

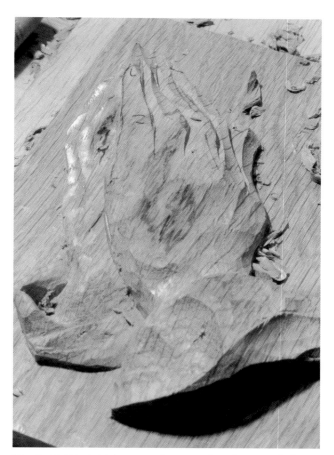

Fig 3.12 Shaping the fingers; the gouge is used 'upside down' in sympathy with the shape that is required

Fig 3.11 The initial stages of carving: big shapes and planes are put in first

MODELLING

When you are satisfied with the overall shape, you can begin refining the planes a little more: dividing the fingers and placing joints, hollowing between the hands (Fig 3.12). It is very important still not to put in details (such as fingernails) yet; just leave rather flat surfaces where the nails will be.

As I point out so often in this book, if you undercut too early there is a danger of removing wood you will need later on. As the shapes begin to become more focused, then they can be worked round and *only then* some undercutting begun (Fig 3.13) and the ground cleaned up underneath.

As the insides of the fingers of the lower hand are visible, these have to be carved in; small shortbent tools are best for this (Fig 3.14). These fingers need to be strongly suggested, but can be left a little vague, or simplified, in comparison with the hand in the foreground.

Fig 3.13 As the hands come into focus, you can begin to work around and underneath the forms

Fig 3.14 Excavating the space between the hands with shortbent tools

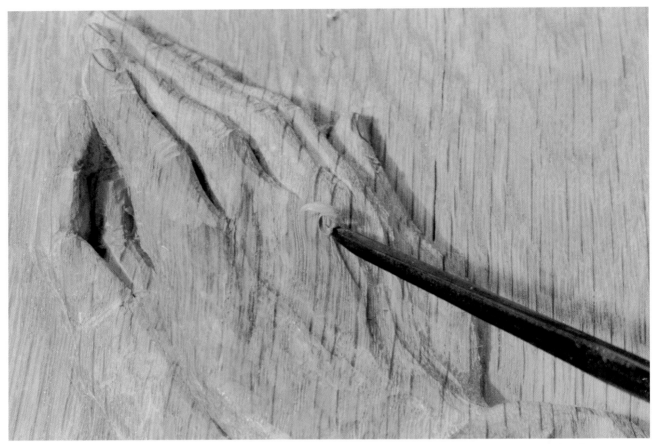

Fig 3.15 *Carving the veins on the backs of the hands. Small details, including fingernails and joint creases, are the last things to carve*

DETAILING

More and more the hands come into focus, and eventually details such as fingernails and veins can be put in.

The nails can be carved with simple crescent cuts to the flattened surface already present.

Veins are carved without hard edges. Use a veiner (a small, deep gouge) to 'lift' the veins from the back of the hand (Fig 3.15), and then slightly lower the surface around them.

The final surface of the hands was finished with flat gouges. There is no need to sand any of the carving if the cutting is clean and sensitive.

A side view of the completed hands (Fig 3.16) shows how the fingers of the lower hand are visible when looked at from the side and therefore need to be included in the carving – as mentioned earlier, this is one of the most important differences between the three-dimensional carving and the two-dimensional drawing.

INITIALS

Finally, Dürer's initials can be added and a simple line border run in with the V-tool (Figs 3.17 and 3.18). As the ground is not flat but slightly tooled, this line appears somewhat irregular, but this is fine and adds to the overall sense of handwork. If a precise line were wanted, then the ground would have to be scraped perfectly flat and a scratch stock used to chase the line. The line serves to reinforce the framing edge of the wood.

FINISH

I slightly darkened the background with two coats of coffee (without milk), a good substitute for true, proprietary stains. The colour contrast threw the hands into even more relief.

The oak was then sealed with a coat of clear shellac, finished with thin beeswax and buffed to a soft polish.

Fig 3.16 *Side view of the completed hands, showing where undercutting is necessary*

Fig 3.18 *Chasing in the framing line with a V-tool*

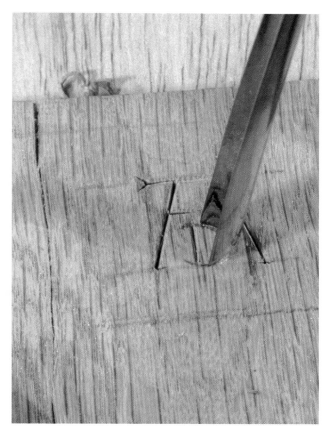

Fig 3.17 *Simple cuts create Albrecht Dürer's initials, taken from another of his works. The hairline shake which appeared in the wood to the left of the monogram was repaired with a sliver of oak, and disappeared when overcarved*

CONCLUSION

Many students want to carve from a drawing or a magazine photograph. This project shows something of the relationship between two-dimensional drawing and three-dimensional carving, and how you have to make a mental 'quantum leap' into a sense of depth.

I wouldn't pretend to have caught more than a shadow of the original, but it was an interesting and enjoyable exercise, causing me to look more closely than I ever would have at this beautiful study of hands by Albrecht Dürer. I still have my initial reservations about using such subjects for carving – and about allowing persuasive nuns into the house. But they were very happy; so was the architect; and, in the end, so was I.

DRAWING

PINNING DOWN ELUSIVE BUTTERFLIES OF THE IMAGINATION

Drawing and modelling are perhaps the most important things to practise, outside of carving itself, for developing your carving skills. At least as many carvings fail through lack of research and preliminary work – such as drawing provides – as lack of skill.

Unfortunately, drawing fills many carving students with dread: they see themselves as 'unartistic' and have never been taught. Usually, however, the problem is more that they have a mistaken idea of what is actually required by us as carvers. For the purposes of woodcarving, drawing is a vital tool for:

- pinning down ideas,
- firming them up into something sensible
- and predicting potential problems;
- taking measurements or cross sections;
- conveying to others what you have in mind;
- helping you visualize during the carving process.

Drawings are a means to an end: the carving. (If you could carve without one, even better – but this skill is unusual even for experienced carvers.) For us, drawings are not meant for display in galleries. However, they will help your carving ability – so give drawing the merit and the time it deserves.

SOME GUIDELINES

- As with carving itself, don't start with the finished product! Sneak up on your final working drawing – and even this need only be a sketch, or a simple outline.

- Get a range of pencils: hard 2H to soft 2B. Hold them lightly, use your wrist – you can pivot on the small wrist bones to make curves – and keep your fingers flexible.

- Start with simple thumbnail sketches, small but in proportion, showing only the main shapes. Rough out many of these until the idea begins to look about right, then increase your size.

- Work very lightly with a hard pencil (2H) to begin with. Strengthen and concentrate your lines (HB–2B) when their position seems right. Use an eraser if you have to, but rub lightly.

- To shade: decide on an imaginary light source (say, top right) and visualize the logical effect this would have. Keep shading (2B) basic and simple: lines, cross-hatching and dots. The purpose of this is to indicate more three-dimensionality to help you visualize – not to create a work of art.

- If your drawing looks a mess, you can trace off the successful lines, using a light box or tracing paper, and start again, or stick a piece of paper over an area and redraw just that section – none of this is 'cheating'!

A WARNING

A two-dimensional drawing is not a three-dimensional carving. *As the depth of a carving increases, so more of the object appears.* And, unlike a drawing, real life doesn't have lines around its hard and soft edges; the outline changes continuously with our viewpoint.

This is the working drawing for the acanthus leaf on page 91; actual height 300mm (12in).
Note that this is only a flat, two-dimensional outline, whereas the finished carving is in three
dimensions. Working drawings do not need to be any neater than this

CHAPTER 4

GREEN MAN 1

I have long been attracted to the images and heads that peer down at us in all our older towns and cities. Look up and around, and you will see classic profiles, bearded gods, monsters, derisive imps with tongues poking out at passers-by. There is a long tradition of placing heads on façades and in churches and, as they look out at us, somewhere in the back of our minds we may sense that behind the controlled 'front' of the world there is another dimension from which they seem to emerge: something uncontrollable, freer, perhaps – definitely more powerful. The Green Man is one such potent image, expressing this tenuous balance between conscious and unconscious forces.

Eventually banned from churches, or relegated to ceilings and corners, the Green Man, in his many forms, is currently re-emerging from the shadows as a meaningful image. A man's face peers out from ebullient foliage, some of which grows from his face, even spews out of his mouth (Fig 4.1). The leaves may perhaps represent creative restlessness, and the

face appears in many different moods: brooding and angry, sad or pensive, light and humorous. It seems as if sculptors through the ages have always given the Green Man a personal interpretation.

Useful books which explore the theme include Kathleen Basford, *The Green Man* (Ipswich: D. S. Brewer, 1978), and William Anderson and Clive Hicks, *Green Man* (London: Harper Collins, 1990).

DESIGN

The Green Man of this project (Fig 4.2) has a somewhat dreamy, somewhat mystical feel, and is an example of the sort of 'solar' image that inhabits the Green Man world alongside the more vigorous and aggressive forces.

DRAWING

I started working out my idea, derived from the many Green Men which I have seen, in rough sketches. From this I made a working drawing of the final head, shown to scale in Fig 4.3.

If you look at the photographs of the carving as it progresses, you will see that the design changed a little from the drawing as I went along. Even though I started with a well-developed drawing, I gave myself permission to deviate from it – to explore the possibilities of balance, and move elements and lines around. This is an important point for carving in general: unless you have a rigorous brief, such as moulding or lettering, keeping a degree of freedom in the design, right from the start, allows you to work around problems and difficulties, or grasp opportunities as they arise. Remember: drawings (and models) are means to an end in carving, not the carving itself.

Fig 4.1 *Late medieval Green Man from Merano, northern Italy*

Fig 4.2 *The finished Green Man project*

Fig 4.3 *Working drawing of half the carving, drawn to scale on a grid of 25mm (1in) squares. The thickness of wood is about 50mm (2in)*

So, by all means work from my drawing if you wish to follow the carving, but remember to follow your own feelings as well. I could have worked from a clay model, but in this case I felt confident enough with just a drawing, being able to visualize the end I wanted to achieve.

There are two strong components to the design: symmetry and concentricity.

BILATERAL SYMMETRY

It matters that the design of the leaves and the face of the Green Man are not absolutely symmetrical – no faces are, and true symmetry looks a little dull and uninteresting. However, the carving wants to 'read' as symmetrical, so that between the two sides there are no awkward changes to interrupt or distract the eye. Even if you were to make the leaves on both sides completely different – as in rococo work – it is important to achieve this sense of the balance of the whole. In this carving there is a bilateral (twofold) symmetry, but that doesn't mean the leaves all have to curl the same way or be of equal thickness.

CONCENTRICITY

The second feature of the design is that, in addition to this symmetry across the mid-line, there is a roughly concentric series of circles (Fig 4.4) with more complexity towards the outside and simplicity towards the centre. The face is kept strong and uncluttered; the lines of the leaves emerge from the face quietly and cleanly, gradually becoming more vigorous towards the edge. The result gives this particular Green Man a solar sense of the 'still eye within the storm', so that the face appears to emerge calmly through the fervent leaves.

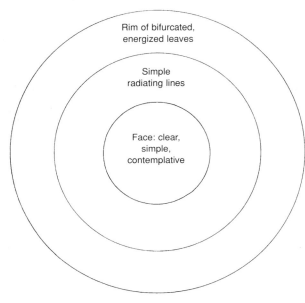

Fig 4.4 *The carving falls roughly into three zones differing in energy and character*

WOOD

I used a piece of English elm. I chose this wood for the 'earthy' feel and colour of the grain: not strong enough to interfere with the lines of the carving, but enough to make the presence of the wood felt. Elm, with its coarse, unpredictable, open grain, will take a similar degree of detail to oak: carving in these woods needs to be strong and simple, with particular use of 'slicing' cuts. Although the leaves may look unsupported and thin at their ends, they are actually quite strong, with only enough undercutting to give them a sense of lightness.

There was a small dead knot in the piece of wood to start with (seen in Fig 4.8). As carving progressed, this unexpectedly developed into a black hole like a rotten tooth – which was unacceptable.

I plugged it with a live knot taken from an offcut of the original fitch, arranging the leaves to camouflage the glue line (see page 42). This worked so well that I feel the need to keep pointing it out!

PREPARING THE BLANK

The lathe is the obvious choice to start off the circular design, but the rounding can be done equally well the long way round with spokeshave and V-tool.

Bandsaw the circle and true it up on the lathe (Fig 4.5). After cleaning off the surface to be carved (but *not* sanding it), run a V-groove round the edge (Fig 4.6) to set the level of the background and produce a small overhang for the leaves.

Fig 4.5 *Turning the initial 405mm (16in) elmwood disc on a faceplate; rounding the edge with a spokeshave would be a more laborious alternative*

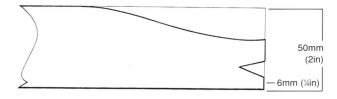

Fig 4.6 *Cross-section of the edge of the wood, after turning; if the blank is being made by hand, use a V-tool to form the groove*

MARKING OUT THE FACE

With the grain vertical, use carbon paper to mark in the face (Figs 4.7 and 4.8) – but *only* the face. The wood carrying the leaves needs to be cut back first, to form the leaves sloping back from the face itself; obviously, any drawing to the side of the face would be removed straight away. So, once the central face has been drawn on the wood, put the piece back on the lathe and skim off material towards the edges of the leaves (as seen already in Fig 4.6). This is in fact part of the roughing-out stage, and if you are not a turner it will need to be done the hard way, with gouge and mallet. The drawing of the leaves themselves can wait until the overall shape towards the edge has been determined.

Fig 4.7 *This side view shows the background level set in with a V-groove, and the tracing paper ready to transfer the design on to the wood*

Fig 4.8 *Only the central features need to be marked in order to start carving*

HOLDING

The circular shape can be held with a simple system of thin, curved blocks and wedges, allowing full access to all the leaves (Fig 4.9). It is a simple matter to knock out the wedges in order to rotate the work as necessary.

Carving vertically using a carver's screw would be my preferred option now, but at this time I was still experimenting with vertical benches.

Fig 4.9 *The work can conveniently be fixed to the bench (or to a separate baseboard) using a system of blocks, wedges and suitably shaped packing pieces*

CARVING

BOSTING IN THE FACE

I always start a carving by deciding on the high points: *the pieces of wood I want to leave*. I prefer to work downhill, from these highest points, into the wood. In this case, the nose and eyebrows would be the most prominent parts, with the cheekbones and lips a little less so; so start by taking wood away down the sides of the nose and into the eye sockets (Fig 4.10).

The levels of the eyes and lips can now be determined (Fig 4.11) and their shapes and positions roughly set in (Fig 4.12). This last photograph shows wood removed from the sides of the forehead and cheekbones, and the face already pushing out of the background. The face itself needs to be convincingly structured – the leaves will emerge out of its anatomy. Drawing a line down the centre, and renewing it whenever it is cut away, will help to keep the balance between the two sides. Dividers can be set from this line if necessary.

Fig 4.10 *Starting to carve away from the highest points*

Fig 4.11 *Nose and eyes beginning to show as the lower levels of the face are pushed back*

Fig 4.12 *With eyes and mouth set in and roughly shaped, the face is beginning to emerge*

ROUGH-CARVING THE LEAVES

Once the face has been 'sketched' in, use carbon paper to draw in the surrounding rim of leaves, adjusting their positions to fit the grain (Fig 4.13).

If you have a drill press or bench drill (see panel on page 29), this can be used to remove some of the waste wood from between the ends of the leaves, ensuring that the holes end at a uniform depth just above the intended background level (Fig 4.14).

Roughly set in the ends of the leaves, *but without undercutting yet* (Fig 4.15). Remember the principle: it is far better to work the form first and let the undercutting follow naturally than risk a mistake by undercutting too early in a carving.

BOSTING IN THE LEAVES

Starting in the middle again, define the wings of the nose, the eyebrows and cheekbones a little more, in preparation for leading off the leaves (Fig 4.16).

Now begin outlining the leaves with a V-tool. Work systematically around the edge, defining and coarsely shaping them – not bifurcating the ends as yet, but simply setting the tone of each one as they sweep outwards. You can use the V-tool, inclined to one side, to separate a leaf from the one below (Fig 4.17); this light degree of undercutting will be sufficient for the central parts of the leaves.

Shape the ends of the leaves with flat gouges (Fig 4.18), aiming to add interest and variety. There should still be a sense of looseness at this stage, but as the forms and positions of the leaves become fixed, so a certain amount of undercutting and cleaning beneath the ends can be started (Fig 4.19).

How and to what extent a particular element should be undercut depends on the position from where the carving is to be viewed (see my *Relief Carving in Wood*, pages 124–5). More undercutting is required on the side of a leaf towards the eye, and less on the other (Fig 4.20). This Green Man was meant to hang a little above eye level. Since undercutting weakens the work, carved elements should be undercut only as much as is necessary to create the illusion of lightness and space beneath.

In Fig 4.19 we saw the bosting in of the leaves partly completed. In this rough stage of carving, the

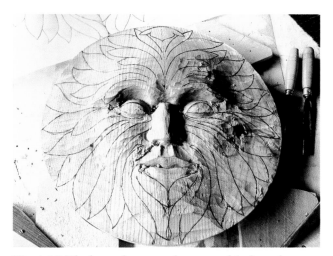

Fig 4.13 *The leaves have now been traced in from the drawing*

Fig 4.14 *Some of the waste wood between the ends of the leaves can be removed by boring*

Fig 4.15 *The ends of the leaves have been simply chopped in to set them in place*

Fig 4.16 *Adding more definition to the wings of the nose*

Fig 4.17 *Using the V-tool to direct the sweeps of the leaves; tilting the tool will give a slight undercut*

Fig 4.18 *Flat gouges are used to give some form and interest to the outer parts of the leaves*

Fig 4.19 The first, rough stage of shaping the leaves, working clockwise from the left. The knot hole is seen on the right

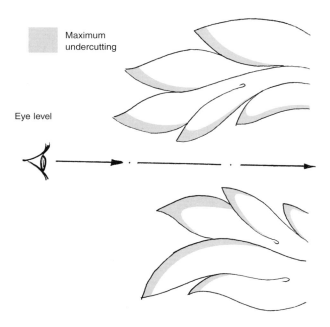

Fig 4.20 The amount of undercutting required at any given point is determined by the eye level at which the carving is designed to be displayed

aim is to set each element in place in relation to the others, and to the underlying movement. Care has to be taken to make the relationship of the leaves and the face logical – for example around the mouth, where the flow of the leaves follows the natural contours and creases of the face. (In this case I chose not to have them emerging directly from the mouth itself.)

REPAIR

The knot hole mentioned previously is clearly visible on the right in Fig 4.19. Once the leaves in this area had been defined, the black hole was bored out and a plug with a more acceptable live knot inserted (Fig 4.21).

Fig 4.22 shows the preliminary roughing-out and bosting-in stages of the carving more or less completed, the work being envisaged as a whole and still left somewhat fluid. I am always relieved when I have got past this stage of a carving and am beginning to know what I am doing!

Fig 4.21 The knot hole bored out and the plug prepared to fill it. A freer style of insert could have been used, but this simple method proved successful

Fig 4.22 The first, rough stage of carving completed; the effect is still rather fluid

MODELLING

In the same systematic way, start refining the surface of the face and eyebrows (Fig 4.23), moving on to the lines of the leaves (Fig 4.24). Aim for smooth, uninterrupted lines. Light fishtail tools become increasingly useful at this stage for working the surfaces, and the skew chisel is helpful for getting into corners (Figs 4.25 and 4.26). V-tools, used with a lifting and rolling motion, help to separate the ends of the leaves.

The most difficult part of the carving is cleaning between and under the ends of the leaves, finishing them down to the background – especially when working the end grain at the top and bottom. To get into these areas comfortably, try holding the carving upright in a vice with padded jaws (Fig 4.27). Provided you use very sharp tools and fine, slicing cuts, you should be able to leave a good surface despite going against the grain.

Fig 4.25 *Using the corner of a fishtail to shape the recesses between the leaves*

Fig 4.23 *Putting a bit more intensity into the eyebrows*

Fig 4.26 *The skew chisel is invaluable for cleaning out acute-angled corners*

Fig 4.24 *Cleaning the lines of the leaves and starting to undercut the edges*

Fig 4.27 *To get at the recesses beneath the leaves, the carving can be held vertically in a vice*

DETAILING

The eyes are set in using appropriately curved gouges (Figs 4.28 and 4.29) – this needs great care so as to get them 'looking right'. Towards the end I played with ideas of defining the iris – until I heard the Green Man telling me not to, but to leave him gazing into infinity. And, of course, you have to listen...

The lips are kept full, with a suggestion of the chin disappearing behind the leaves (Fig 4.30).

FINISHING

Sandpaper is not necessary on this carving: clean cuts and long strokes give a lovely, textured surface which enhances the flow of the leaves (Figs 4.31 and 4.32). As you approach the end of the carving, try changing the lighting completely, even taking the work outside for a close inspection – this can be surprisingly revealing.

You will need to make some provision for hanging the carving on the wall; I chose a brass escutcheon plate (Fig 4.33).

My carving was sealed with a coat of clear shellac; then thin, followed by thicker, beeswax, brushed in. Linseed oil would have made the elmwood turn a lot darker, particularly if exposed to sunlight. The wood polished up with a brush to a beautiful brown colour (Fig 4.34).

CONCLUSION

I know that many students and readers of *Woodcarving* magazine (where this carving first appeared) have made their own versions of this Green Man, so I can assume it has been well received. Some have put in pupils; some have followed my lead and left the eyes vacant. Every now and then I pencil in irises for carving, but then rub them out again. I think their absence disturbs me, but I suppose this must be the 'crunch' of the design.

Fig 4.28 The shape of the eye is refined by slicing cuts with gouges of matching curvature

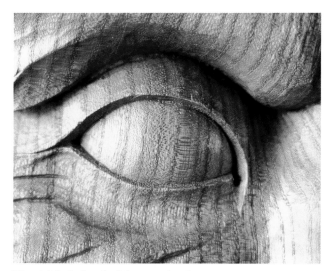

Fig 4.29 A detail of the completed eye

Fig 4.30 Detail of the mouth. The curl of the leaves needs to suggest the shape of the chin beneath

Fig 4.31 *The finishing stage involves refining the surface with sharp carving tools, so that abrasives will not be needed*

Fig 4.32 *The textured surface left by the tool cuts would have been spoilt by sanding*

Fig 4.33 *The escutcheon plate used to hang the carving*

Fig 4.34 *The finished carving in elm: not too much grain to confuse the details, but enough to emphasize the woody origins of the Green Man*

MODELLING

DRAWING IN SPACE

Here I mean modelling with soft, plastic material such as clay, rather than the other sense of 'modelling' which I use elsewhere: more sensitive fashioning of the wood with carving tools after the bosting-in stage.

It is rare to find experienced carvers starting a complicated carving (perhaps in the round) without first making many drawings, and a model in clay or Plasticine. Like drawing, modelling is only a means to an end – the carving – and what is needed is often misunderstood by beginners. The following thoughts may help.

PURPOSE

- **Pinning down an idea**: as a drawing does, but three-dimensionally. A drawing has one viewpoint; a model can have them all.

- **Measuring**: establishing what dimensions of wood are needed; what large initial volumes of waste wood can be safely bandsawn from the block at an early stage; and for a reference as the work continues.

- **Early problem-solving**: establishing wood strength and grain direction, and generally as an *aide-mémoire* to 'how things work'.

TOOLS AND MATERIALS

- Clay, Plasticine, children's modelling clay, etc. are very readily available and cheap. Nuclay, which hardens in air, is particularly useful.

- **Tools**: Start with your fingers; make simple tool shapes from hardwood as you need them, or buy them from art shops.

PRACTICE

- Don't take your modelling too seriously – be light!

- Get one of the many books available to give you advice on storing clay, keeping it wet, etc.

- Begin with simple shapes. Don't go straight for a complicated design without building up your confidence and competence first – you'll only be disappointed.

- Modelling builds *from the inside out*. Try and build up main masses first, then add smaller lumps in the directions you want to go; towards the end you will be adding very small pieces.

- Cut back if, you have to, with wire tools.

- If you just push into the clay in one place, it will simply push out in another. Avoid pushing; rather, add and subtract.

- Keep the clay damp and consolidate the surface with a soft, wet brush.

- You need only bring the model to the stage where the idea of your carving is fixed in your mind, or you have studied your subject in enough detail to make a start on the carving. Even if you discard your model after the modelling session, you will still have gone a long way towards achieving its purpose.

Life-size king's head in Nuclay – the model on which the carving on pages 25 and 59 is based. This is a complicated carving: the crown in particular needs to be worked out carefully. The model helped solve many problems

PITFALLS

Clay models and woodcarvings are different beasts. The process of modelling (a **plastic** process) is entirely unlike and distinct from carving (a **glyptic** process) – in the material, the tools, the technique and so on. The result should reflect this. Don't just make a model and then copy it in wood. Use it while you need to, then work with the carving only as soon as you can.

CHAPTER 5

GREEN MAN 2

The Green Man, whether in his light or dark form, comes from the same source as all our deep myths; and since the Green Man archetype in its wide variety of forms has been around since before Dionysus, it must be here to stay.

I don't think it at all a coincidence that the image of Man-with-Nature arises strongly in these times, reinterpreted by woodcarvers and other artists; and since carvers in stone and wood have been the main keepers of the flame, it is not surprising that we should be drawn to carve it, or find it so popular a subject. This version (Fig 5.1) is a deeper and a leafier image than that in the previous chapter. The vital point is that we carvers must keep exploring, trying to bring about our own images of the Green Man. So, if you do follow this project, also feel free to follow your heart's inclinations and inspirations and make the image your own, rather than simply copying it.

DESIGN

The request from the client was for a Green Man with a benign but mischievous expression, large and deep – and no regurgitating leaves, thank you. The design I created is 'stylized' in the sense that I have altered nature to my own ends: in the shape of the mouth and the leaves, for example.

I was not particularly interested in representing an actual species of leaf, nor carving them in detail. The leaves are meant to fall somewhere between fig and oak (would this be a 'folk' leaf?). The intention was to leave them a little 'out of focus', so that the observer's eye would be continually drawn to meet the eyes of the carving, which I spaced a little wide.

Fig 5.1 *The finished carving in English oak, 450 x 350mm (18 x 14in), 135mm (5¼in) deep*

MODEL AND DRAWING

The drawing (Fig 5.2) is actually taken from a model that I made first in Nuclay. The model was about half-size, scaled to the proportions of the wood I had in mind (Fig 5.3).

I suspended a piece of thick glass over the high relief model and traced the design on to the glass with a Chinagraph pencil. To avoid perspective distortion, I sighted along a metal try square to ensure a consistent viewpoint (Fig 5.4).

Fig 5.2 *My working drawing for the carving*

Fig 5.3 *The Nuclay model from which I started*

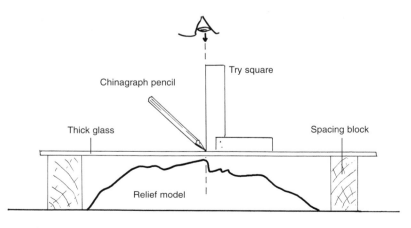

Fig 5.4 *Tracing the working drawing from the model. Eyeing along the try square as it moved around the profile greatly reduced the risk of distortion*

The glass drawing then went on to my light box and was transferred to paper. I checked for adequate symmetry, especially around the face, and arrived at a final working drawing. I got the drawing to the exact size I wanted with a photocopier.

Although I often have a model or a working drawing to start with, I always feel that the sooner I can dispense with them, and work directly on my piece of wood, the better. *Drawings, or models, are not woodcarvings.* Everything about these media – their three-dimensionality (or lack of it), the tools and methods of working them, their overall impact – is different (see Drawing on page 34 and Modelling on pages 46–7). See them as helping you off in the right direction, giving you an idea of wood size and preliminary waste, but be very aware, as you carve, that you are not drawing or modelling.

WOOD

I had some lovely air-dried English oak of the right thickness, overlong, but not wide enough. I have always favoured elm and oak for Green Men – the more 'woody'-looking the material, the better.

JOINING

I took the extra length, split it and glued the parts to either side of the main block (Fig 5.5). This gave me a maximum overall starting size: height 450mm (18in); width 350mm (14in); and thickness 135mm (5¼in). It was to this size that I enlarged the drawing, so getting the most I could out of the wood.

As a rule, the worst place to put a join in a face is symmetrically, down the nose; the eye is very sensitive to symmetry. Although the join to the right in Fig 5.1 is fairly conspicuous because of the darker grain, the whole piece darkened quickly after this early photograph was taken, and the contrast is now hardly visible.

HOLDING

Carving this heavy relief is a suitable project for the tilting bench surface described in Chapter 2 (pages 16–19). The more vertical position gives a better

Fig 5.5 *The three pieces of wood after joining. The main lines of the drawing have been transferred to the wood with carbon paper, ready for preliminary shaping. I like to start off with clean surfaces where possible*

view when you step back. A carver's screw through a slot in the surface allows the work to be raised or lowered, or turned upside down for undercutting the lower leaves. If you place the screw hole in the back where the hanging plate will go, it will disappear in the finished piece.

The carver's screw is the ideal answer because, once the preliminary shape begins to appear, there is nowhere to clamp. Gluing the carving to a board (paper-sandwich method) is an option, as is screwing a block to the back to go in the vice. However, problems then arise with the undercutting: for this you need to find a method (such as a coach bolt and thick post) which enables you to get at the sides easily.

CARVING

ROUGHING OUT

Having transferred the drawing to the wood with carbon paper and bandsawed the profile, the

Fig 5.6 *The head bandsawn to shape, and waste removed with an Arbortech*

quickest way to rough in the main shape is with a power-carving tool such as the Arbortech. Fig 5.6 shows how far this stage can be taken before switching to ordinary carving tools.

BOSTING IN

You will find that the carving work divides itself into three phases:

1. The face: this can be almost finished before beginning on

2. the leaves extending outwards; then as the leaves are completed you can tackle

3. the deep undercutting, beneath and around the sides of the leaves.

As lines disappear, redraw them; I redrew them to my liking rather than following the drawing. It is worth keeping the centre line.

Most of the rough work can be done with three large gouges – flat, medium and deep (nos. 3, 6, 9), all 38mm (1½in) wide – and a 25mm (1in) V-tool.

ROUGHING IN THE FACE

First note the high spots – in other words, where you *don't* want to remove wood. The main place is the tip of the nose, but others, such as cheekbones and forehead, will soon become apparent.

From these high places the carving can be swept down into the leaves (Fig 5.7). Two points are important here:

Fig 5.7 *Beginning the rough shaping with gouges, sweeping down from the high points into the leaves. The centre line is worth keeping to help with symmetry of the face*

1. Since the face is made of leaves, the leaves themselves must be bent or shaped to show its structure – cheek bones, temple bones (to the sides of the forehead) and throat – and to create the helmet-like furrowing of the brow (Fig 5.8). This needs to be borne in mind continually as you create the shapes of the leaves.

Fig 5.8 *The eye sockets have been pushed back, and mouth and nose are taking shape. The sweep of the leaves is used to describe the features and the furrowing of the brow*

2　A practical point: with a mallet and these large gouges, work proceeds vigorously. As you come to the outside edge of the wood, the fibres are less supported by material beyond, and the danger is that end pieces fracture off. So, as you approach any edge in the wood, stop short and reverse direction, cutting *into* the wood mass so that the fibres are well supported.

MODELLING THE FACE

Once the main masses are in place, with their direction and flow established, it is time to start dividing these into smaller masses: the wings of the nose, the mouth, the balls of the eye. It doesn't happen as neatly as this in practice, but you must be careful of fixing too much, or putting in detail which really belongs to the final stages. All parts are relative to others, so by all means take reference points, but try and keep loose. You will see from the photographs how parts change as the forms firm up, or come into focus.

MOUTH

In Fig 5.9 the mouth has been more or less placed and the corners are being pushed back. Smaller gouges are needed now. To form the ends of the lips, the leaves arising from the side of the nose have to be undercut. For this you need tightly cranked shortbent (spoon-bit) gouges; and it is in this sort of work – tight, deep hollows – that shortbents really come into their own. Nothing else will do to get the clean cuts needed here without resorting to high-speed cutters. Many shortbent tools are made with a rather slight bend that gives only a small advantage over the straight tool. Few manufacturers make what are known as 'knuckle' gouges as part of their normal range, and I had to go to Henry Taylor Ltd especially for the knuckle V-tool shown in Fig 5.10.

An 'eye' (a small circular hole) can be cut at the outermost point of the lips, as a way of ending them, by rotating a small no. 9 (semicircular) gouge. The wood should pop out, and the eye can eventually be deepened with a punch.

Fig 5.9 *Forming the outer limit to the lips; an 'eye' has been marked to indicate where the parting of the lips should end, but the shape is far from right yet*

You can also see in Fig 5.10 how the cut surfaces can be kept clean as you work by pushing the waste into corners and recesses which are then cleaned up. This allows the work to progress towards the final surface without too much effort. I wasn't intending to sand this piece, but even if I had been I would have wanted to get as near to a finished surface as possible with the carving tools.

You will notice that the shape of the end of the mouth at this stage (with the 'eye' drawn in) is

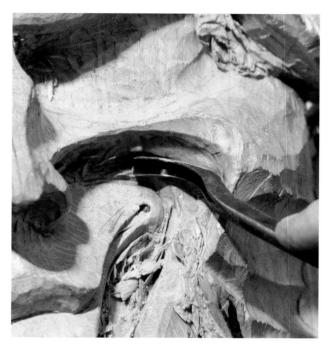

Fig 5.10 *Working in the tight recess near the corner of the mouth with a sharply bent or 'knuckle' V-tool*

Fig 5.12 *Shaping the eyeball and lower lid. The shape of the end of the lips has been improved and the 'eye' redrawn*

different from its later appearance. This is because the lower lip was subsequently taken back as wood around it was removed. Fig 5.11 shows the final shape of the mouth as well as the nose. All the tool marks are subtle, but clearly visible.

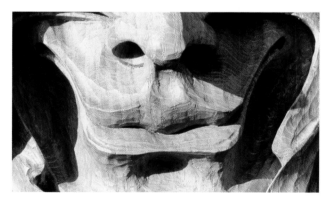

Fig 5.11 *Detail of the completed nose and lips. Note the strong changes of plane and the strong contrasts of light and dark resulting from them*

EYES

The eyes in any face are probably the most critical feature. Again, the important thing here is to create the shape of the eyeballs and surrounding structures first (Fig 5.12); then the irises and pupils will

naturally fall into place. It is common for newcomers to carving to put in the pupils first and work back from these. This is understandable because it is the pupils which seem to be looking at you, but it is a mistake. *The rule in carving is to put in the larger underlying forms first – the details will naturally follow.*

Fig 5.13 shows this area finished. The eyebrow is again deeply undercut. There are several ways of forming the iris and pupil, or you may prefer not to do so at all – in the previous chapter I left the eyes of the Green Man blank altogether.

Fig 5.13 *The finished eye. The brow is strong and somewhat helmet-like*

Get the shape of the eyeball first; remember it is a ball and recedes in all directions from a point. The outline of the iris is a groove carved with an appropriately sized semicircular (no. 9) gouge – in this way you can be sure that they are the same size on each side.

The pupil is heart-shaped: the idea is that the little nib at the top catches the light and reflects in the way a normal eye does. Make an 'eye' hole, as before, on either side of the nib, then join the holes together to make the heart shape with a scoop from a larger gouge.

NOSE

The nose (Fig 5.14) is fairly straightforward, as it has already been given some shape early on. Remember not to undercut into the nostrils until you are absolutely confident that the wings of the nose are where you want them to be. I made the bone of the nose a strong feature. Note how the leaves take off from the wings of the nose and form a sort of 'cheek-plate' that represents the shape of the cheekbones themselves (Fig 5.15).

Fig 5.15 Detail of the face. All the lines are strong and flowing, and the surfaces clean. Note how the shape of the cheekbones is suggested by the covering leaves

LEAVES

While carving the face, you will have been unavoidably pushing away the leaves and roughly shaping them. Now it is their turn for shaping and final modelling, followed by undercutting (Figs 5.16 and 5.17). I left the surfaces tooled, but with the veins no more than implied. At one time I did experiment with adding veins, but I felt this distracted from the face.

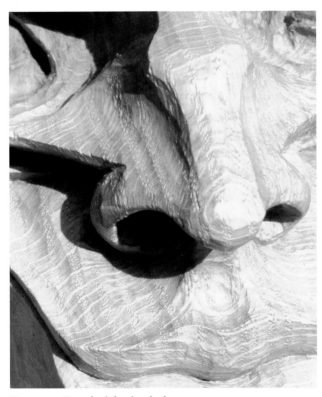

Fig 5.14 Detail of the finished nose

Fig 5.16 Shaping the leaves. There is much undercutting to be done at the sides, and it is possible to do some of this with the bandsaw and the Arbortech

Fig 5.17 *Finished leaf surfaces. A glue line is faintly visible in the uppermost leaf*

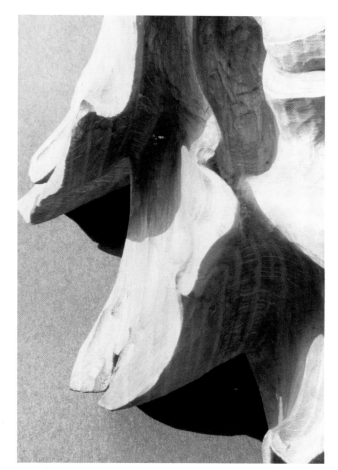

Fig 5.18 *An angled view of the chin area demonstrates the shadows created by the undercutting*

UNDERCUTTING

All surfaces can be left from the chisel. This requires immaculately sharp cutting edges and, as we saw earlier on, a habit of clean cutting from the start – *cleaning up as you go along.*

The undercutting will probably take as long as the rest of the carving, but is necessary if the shadows are to be strong and the overall effect a bit dramatic (Fig 5.18). Leave buttresses for strength, and don't make the edges too thin and weak.

Undercutting can be quite hard work, and requires patience to get the surfaces as clean behind the leaves as in front – people always look! There is extensive undercutting to the upper leaves that cannot be seen in the photographs. Fig 5.19 gives some indication of the depth of undercutting. Being able to turn the work round to get clear access to the back is vital.

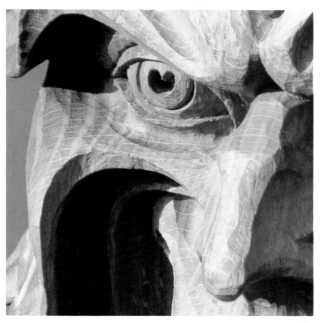

Fig 5.19 *An oblique view showing the depth of undercutting around the cheeks and eye sockets*

REPAIR

A small 'shake' or crack appeared in the end grain at the top, behind the upper leaves. This sometimes happens as the wood in a carving 'settles down' to its new distribution of material masses. Although in this case the damage was not apparent from the front, it was worth repairing because this sort of end-grain split is easy to deal with; Figs 5.20–5.22 show the procedure. Use wedge-shaped slivers of wood taken from offcuts of the original block, matching the colour carefully. Tap them in with glue, pare them off carefully and recarve the surface. The result is usually invisible.

Fig 5.21 The protruding ends of the wedges are pared away carefully with a chisel

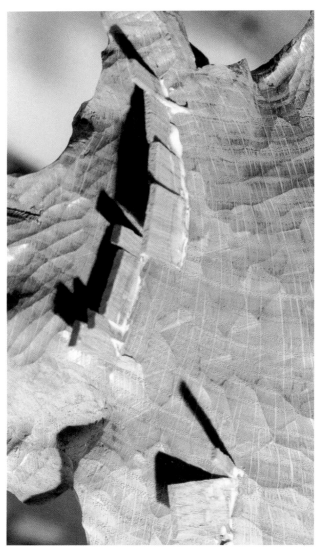

Fig 5.20 Wedge-shaped slivers of matching wood have been inserted into the crack

Fig 5.22 Once it has been gone over again with a gouge, the finished surface has no visible cracks

FINISHING

A keyhole plate is attached at the back for hanging the carving, and this also serves to conceal the hole left by the carver's screw. The back is sealed with shellac. The front has several thin coats of beeswax (with a little carnauba wax), brushed on and burnished. I never wax the back of a carving that will lie against a wall, as this may leave greasy spots on the wall.

CONCLUSION

I think the good size and depth, the balance of woody colour and feel and mischievous personality work well; and certainly the clients were happy with how I had interpreted their wishes. I think if I did a second version I would make the eyes and mouth narrower and push the nose out more, like an aquiline beak – but then Green Men are endless.

JOINING WOOD

TRADITION AND FASHION

It may be thought that joining wood for carving is somehow a poor way of working, implying that the carver couldn't find a single piece the right size. This may actually be true. Then again, some think joints in themselves are a 'bad thing'. But joining wood is part of the long woodcarving and woodworking tradition; it's what you do with wood, and for carving, joining up has only recently gone out of fashion in favour of single blocks. Think of the huge numbers of old carvings that are admired, but the joints hardly remarked on.

WHY JOIN WOOD?

- Because you cannot get the necessary bulk in a single piece.

- **For economy**: the waste from a whole log may be more than what is actually used – time can also be saved.

- **For strength**: it allows the grain to be run into weak parts.

- **For stability**: thinner wood can be seasoned more thoroughly.

- For the sake of colour or other effects.

APPEARANCE

It may be that a carving really is best without any joints; but if you have them, the trick is to make the joints unobtrusive. This means:

- placing the joints carefully, where they will be least visible (See Chapter 5, where joins are placed among the side leaves and away from the face, and Chapter 8, where they are concealed in the folds of the shirt);

- making good, close joints;

- matching the colour and figuring as closely as possible;

- colouring the glue if necessary, particularly if you are staining the wood.

If a glue line is in too obvious a place, then redesign.

HOW TO JOIN WOOD

- Study how to do it. I discussed some aspects in *Woodcarving Tools, Materials & Equipment* (page 327), but it is a skill in its own right and does need to be thoroughly learned if it is going to be most useful and successful.

- You can flatten joint faces in many ways, using plane, planer-surfacer, router, belt sander, sandpaper glued to a flat board – it depends on the work. Immaculate joins can be made by hand, but it does need practice.

- Understand the effect of movement between your pieces of wood.

- Choose your type of glue carefully. Is it for indoor or outdoor use? Superglue, for example, is only (and supremely) useful for minor repairs; hot-melt glue is good for tacking work down temporarily, but not for joints.

SOME PRINCIPLES

- Glue in itself has no strength. If it is being used to fill spaces in the joint, that is *all* it will do.

- Wood surfaces should be as close-fitting as possible to give maximum grain contact.

- Make sure your wood is properly dry: only certain specialist glues will work on damp wood.

- Pressure is essential to get proper glue penetration: harder, thicker woods need more than soft, thinner ones. Wood prepared on a planer or jointer has a finely rippled surface, and pressure is needed to increase the amount of contact between the two surfaces.

Close up of the King's head in oak shown on page 25, and based on the model on page 47. This carving is made up of six pieces of wood, laminated together. The joints are almost invisible

CHAPTER 6

PADMASAMBHAVA

The subject of this relief carving (Fig 6.1) has an extremely important place in Tibetan Buddhist culture and history. As one of Tibet's most famous and revered spiritual teachers, Padmasambhava is said to have brought the teachings of the Buddha to Tibet in the eighth century of the Christian era.

With time, his life and the Buddhist teachings mingled with the indigenous animist religion, with the result that the personality of Padmasambhava took on an archetypal significance, entering Tibetan mythology as one who fights demons and performs miracles, and whose teachings have the power to move practitioners beyond themselves.

DESIGN

I have represented Padmasambhava in the aspect of an uncompromising teacher, richly dressed and enthroned on a lotus. In traditional iconography the figure of Padmasambhava is portrayed in several different forms; in particular, he is to be found in Tibetan paintings called *Thangkas* where layer upon layer of symbolism is included as an *aide-mémoire* for contemplation and as direct material for meditation.

It is this emphasis on symbolism which, while very important to include in the carving, at the same time caused me some problems in the design. There are many Thangka paintings from which one might take inspiration, but these all tend to be heavy with detail (Fig 6.2), and it is far easier to paint such details than to

Fig 6.1 *The finished relief carving of Padmasambhava in jelutong, 740 x 680mm (29 x 26½in), 32mm (1¼in) thick*

Fig 6.2 *Detail from* Tibetan Thangka Painting *by David and Janice Jackson (Serindia Publications, 1984), page 63, showing Padmasambhava's right foot. Such drawings are meant as a guide to painting; for carving I had to find a simpler way to express the same thing, and this excellent volume was just one of the many books I had to research.*

have to carve them. For example, as the meaning of Padmasambhava's name in Sanskrit is 'Lotus-Born', he is often shown seated on a lotus, hanging in space – all of which has important symbolic meaning. Illustrations very often show this lotus to have literally thousands of petals and, while this would not be *impossible* to carve, I felt such elaboration was more suitable to painting than carving – never mind the cost!

So I simplified here, as elsewhere, seeking to find a balance between pedagogic iconography and the personal interpretation of symbolism. It was a challenge which I was pleased to undertake, and I hope that, in the end, the carving conveys something of the presence and tone of the original image. I will mention some of the symbolism along the way, as I describe the carving itself.

In the design of the carving I tried to balance parts in which a lot is going on – in terms of rhythms and detailed areas – with other parts having a feeling of space (see Fig 6.9).

WOOD

Using simple but accurate butt joints, I assembled a panel in jelutong measuring 740 x 680mm (29 x 26½in), with a thickness of 32mm (1¼in). The background ended up about 10mm (⅜in) thick, making the depth of carving about 22mm (⅞in).

Illustrations of Padmasambhava are usually brightly coloured; but this is a woodcarving, and as such communicates only by light and shadow. I chose jelutong because of its capacity for detail, and its warm honey colour.

Jelutong often has latex channels which can be both disfiguring and unexpected. I knew about the small ones in my material, and my approach was to ignore such defects until the end of the carving. I then repaired them using the particularly successful method described on pages 65–6.

HOLDING

I clamped the workpiece to the near-vertical surface of the tilting bench described in Chapter 2. Sometimes I turned the work upside down or on to one side to get better access.

DRAWING

The design that I had worked out was transferred to the panel with carbon paper, but while I was carving I found that the ink rubbed off on to my hands and caused surrounding wood to become grubby. I solved this by sticking the initial drawing on to the panel with masking tape and carving straight through it (see Fig 6.6).

CARVING

This project is a relief carving, and as such can be interestingly compared with the simpler carving of the Hands in Chapter 3.

ROUGHING OUT

In terms of a relief carving, 'roughing out' could be said to include the removing of the background waste prior to carving the subject itself. This is more strictly termed **grounding** or **grounding out**, and has three stages:

1 lowering or removing surrounding waste,

2 levelling and cleaning up the background,

3 setting in the outline of the subject.

LOWERING THE BACKGROUND AND SHAPING THE FRAME

The purpose of the lowering stage is to remove as much of the background waste as possible, and for this the plunging router is ideal.

Start with the frame of the carving, using a fence on the machine. As you can see in Fig 6.1, elements of the figure actually break into the frame – this breaking of boundaries is itself symbolic – and you will have to be particularly mindful not to rout through these areas.

For this sort of wasting work, a variety of straight bits in various sizes will allow you to come close to the lines of the drawing. Remember to leave spare wood for the sun and moon in the background.

The technique of lowering and levelling backgrounds with hand tools is discussed in detail in my *Relief Carving in Wood: A Practical Introduction* (pages 51–6 and 77–85).

Both the outside and inside of the frame can be moulded with a moulding cutter on the router; where elements of the carving overlap the frame, finish off neatly around and up to them with appropriate carving tools.

LEVELLING

Flatten and clean up the ground with a large flat gouge (no. 3, or Swiss no. 2). Eventually 'aura' lines will be chased in with a V-tool, but not until the final stage of the carving.

SETTING IN

Actually, very little of this is needed. The normal method in relief carving is to set in the outline of the subject fairly accurately and then shape it (see chapters 4 and 5 of my *Relief Carving in Wood*). However, a more efficient way to proceed – although one which needs more confidence and ability to foresee the underlying forms – is to shape the subject first and *then* set in. Various photographs in this chapter show this process. So, after levelling the background we can go straight into the figure.

THE FIGURE

BOSTING IN

Padmasambhava is portrayed richly enrobed, with wild, long hair and piercing eyes. He confronts the viewer with threatening images, urging people to make an effort and transform their lives before death sweeps them away; yet at the heart of this he also promises a way. I knew that the face would dictate most of the mood of the finished piece and that if I wasn't happy with it then I wouldn't feel much for the rest of the carving. So I got the face going well first (Fig 6.3), before tackling the rest of the figure.

As we saw earlier (Notes on the Carving Process, page 24), carving needs a disciplined approach, which entails at least two general principles:

1   A carving is best tackled *as a whole*. While it is true that I went against this rule by starting with

the head, I remained aware of the whole figure and then went on to work the rest of the carving as a whole.

2   Carve the main masses or forms first: this is the purpose of the bosting or sketching stage.

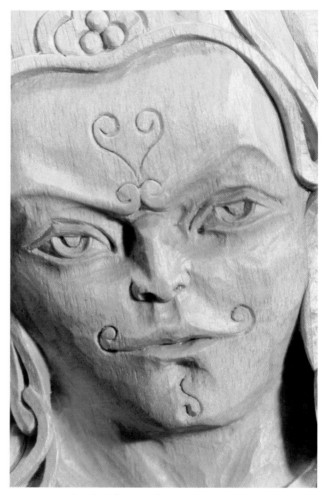

Fig 6.3 *A detail of the completed face*

Some of the photographs show these two principles in action. For example, Fig 6.4 shows an earlier stage in which the main masses of the background banners are beginning to shape up; Fig 6.5 is same area in the finished carving.

Fig 6.6 shows a preliminary stage where the main forms of hand and sleeve have been placed in position; Fig 6.7 is the same area of carving, finished. The hand holds a 'skull cup' overflowing with blood and containing a fiery 'vase of initiation': a promise and reminder to practitioners of alternative ways of being.

Fig 6.4 *An early stage of bosting in, where main masses such as the banners are in position. Note the latex pocket in the hat, which became practically invisible after repair with a Dutchman*

Fig 6.5 *The same area, finished*

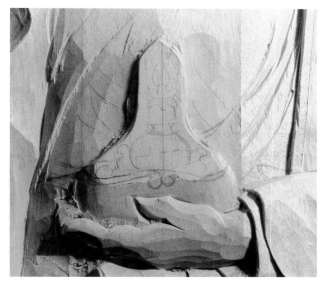

Fig 6.6 *The left hand at an early stage. Note how the carbon paper drawing has been masked to prevent the ink smudging; even pencil lines can make the carving look grimy*

Fig 6.7 *The same area, finished. Punches have been used to decorate the edges of the robe and the inner garment*

MODELLING

When the main masses have been put in, they can be subdivided into lesser ones; this can be seen in Fig 6.8, where layers of the robe are visible and details of the necklace are being drawn in. Fig 6.9 is the same area of neck, finished.

One of the most complicated parts of the carving was that of the staff held by Padmasambhava's right arm (Figs 6.10 and 6.11). The top part was pierced beneath, so as to lie clear of the background. It retains strength from the frame and from the orientation of the grain, which runs upwards and along the staff.

This staff is actually a flaming trident, and the heads represent the mortal nature of human beings. The forceful imagery is meant to provoke the viewer into considering deeply the human lot. Padmasambhava is not a sort of 'gentle Jesus, meek and mild' figure, and Westerners are sometimes shocked by the use of such strong imagery in Tibetan iconography. However, to shock is sometimes entirely the point, and one needs to remember that these are all iconographic symbols, and each has to be taken as only part of the whole picture.

Fig 6.8 *The main planes of the carving have to be put in place first, then the detail will naturally fall into position*

Fig 6.9 *The same area, finished. The difference in tone across the join is likely to diminish after a while as the wood mellows in colour. Long and exotic earrings are a sign of wealth and the princely qualities of Padmasambhava*

Fig 6.10 *Padmasambhava's flaming trident extends into the frame at the top of the carving*

Fig 6.11 *Detail of the three heads on the trident*

DETAILS

Modelling naturally develops into detailing, and sometimes it is hard to say where one stage ends and the other begins.

As the finish is to be left from the cutting edges, dirty wood can only be removed by recarving. I actually went to a great deal of trouble to keep the carving clean, jelutong being prone to dirtying easily. For example, I covered the carving in between sessions, and parts of it during sessions; I also rested my carving hands on clean paper, taped to the wood and moved around as necessary (see Clean Work on page 90).

You can see the tool marks in Fig 6.8 and elsewhere. I tried to get them to 'mean' something, in the sense of defining changes of plane or following the direction of the form.

What appears to be a pierced rosette in Fig 6.10 is in fact a crossed or double *vajra*; Fig 6.12 shows a single vajra. As a ritual implement, the vajra is ubiquitous in Tibetan Buddhism. The word means 'thunderbolt' or 'diamond', and it is a symbol of both the direct experience of enlightenment, and the power to attain it. I have stylized what is actually a far more complicated device, piercing the wood to give it more impact in the design.

Fig 6.12 The right hand holds a ritual device known as a vajra *in a specific gesture. The simple drapery balances the more detailed carving elsewhere*

There are many other passages where some simplification is needed in order to translate the elaborate forms of Tibetan iconography into wood: compare, for example, the right foot as I carved it (Fig 6.13) with the drawn version shown in Fig 6.2.

Fig 6.13 The right foot, represented in much less detail than the elaborate version shown in Fig 6.2

In other photographs you can see the use of punches to suggest an embroidered inner garment, and for decoration on the outer edges of the robes. This punching is a final effect, applied to a cleanly finished surface.

REPAIRS

When the carving was completed, there was still the matter of the few latex channels to be repaired. My method involves inserting a plug of wood, which I know as a 'Dutchman', into a pre-cut hole over the defect. Why it is called a Dutchman, where this term comes from, whether it's abusive to the Dutch, or even where I got the term in the first place, I have no idea. The shape of the Dutchman merges well into carved work, better than a circular plug.

THE TECHNIQUE

1 Cut a series of boat-shaped inserts from a carefully grain-matched piece of wood using a medium-sweep gouge (Fig 6.14). Make the Dutchmen oversize and slightly tapered, so that when tapped in with a hammer they give an almost invisible glue line. Even better, dry the wood so that it swells in its hole as it absorbs moisture from the glue.

2 Then, *using the same gouge*, stab in carefully around the defect in the carving (Fig 6.15).

3 Use small shortbent skew chisels to clean out the waste, and you should end up with a neat complementary hole (Fig 6.16).

4 Tap in the plug, using PVA or other wood adhesive (Fig 6.17).

5 Finally, carve away the surplus wood – in this case so as to re-level the background (Fig 6.18).

Fig 6.16 *Use a small shortbent skew to remove the waste*

Fig 6.14 *Use a medium gouge to make the Dutchmen, which should taper very slightly*

Fig 6.17 *Glue the Dutchman and tap it home*

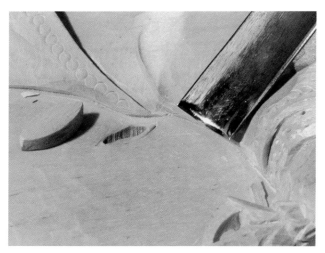

Fig 6.15 *Use the same gouge to delineate the hole which cuts away the defect*

Fig 6.18 *Pare off the waste and carve over the patch. The shape of the repair makes it merge unobtrusively into the carving*

FINISHING

I give a good treatment of anti-woodworm preservative to all my carvings. In this case it was especially important: the carving was a commission for a Buddhist centre in Britain, but may well find its way to another centre in Venezuela. The owner is concerned about a ravenous Venezuelan moth which makes the eating habits of our woodworm seem positively frugal.

The final finish was several thin coats of thin beeswax, to which a small amount of carnauba wax had been added, put on and burnished with brushes.

CONCLUSION

Although appearing pale in the photographs, the wood has since matured to a lovely colour. The carving lacks the impact of a highly coloured painting, but still comes over as a strong image.

I would say that at least a third of the time in this carving went into the designing, joining and other preparatory work, rather than actual carving. This is an interesting and important point when it comes to costing work. It is not inconceivable that more time may be spent not carving than carving.

CLEAN CUTTING

SLICING AND POLICING

The surface of a carving is what you see, and often what you touch. It can be smoothly sanded or left straight from the tool. This is not a moral choice, a 'right' or 'wrong', but a choice which carvers should be able to make consciously and in keeping with their intentions.

The reality is, however, that many students and aspiring carvers are not in a position to exercise real choice, and end up *having* to sand because they cannot cut cleanly and leave a lightly tooled surface; they don't really know how to. But it's actually quite simple, and essentially a question of adopting a habitual and disciplined way of working right from the start.

THE BASIC SLICING CUT

The slicing cut is what you need, and it is used in all the projects in this book. With this method you can actually cut 'uphill', against the grain, and this will enable you to deal with even the most intractable grain surfaces.

- Keep the corners of the tool clear of the wood surface to avoid digging in.

- As the carving tool is pushed forwards into the wood, slice across with the cutting edge:

- with a flat gouge, this means a slight rotation and a 'drifting' or pulling (or pushing) of the blade across the line of cut;

- with a deeper gouge, more rotation of the handle is needed to make the edge slice as it cuts.

The slicing cut is described and demonstrated in further detail in my *Lettercarving in Wood* (page 129), and *Relief Carving in Wood* (page 55).

PRINCIPLES

- It goes without saying that you must have keen tools whose edges do not leave rough trails ('snail tracks') in the wood.

- Both front and back hands must work together to control the tool.

- Learn to slice to the right or left easily at will, and as the lie of the grain dictates.

- Get into the habit of slicing and cutting cleanly even in the early bosting-in stages – whenever you are using hands rather than a mallet.

- Think of the process as paring or 'pushing back' a surface to reveal what's underneath.

'Police' the area as you work: don't leave torn surfaces, thinking you'll come back to them later – you won't. *Clean up as you go along.*

Painted face of a half-life-size St Francis from an Italian atelier, late 20th century. Left from the chisel, the cleanly finished surface of this face is soft and flesh-like. Imperfections, such as on the left lower eyelid and in the wings of the nose, probably resulted from this carving being produced at speed – but thanks to the confidence of the carver these 'blemishes' only add to the character of the face

CHAPTER 7

IKARUS

Woodcarving is a wide field – very wide indeed, with an almost limitless choice of approaches for artists and carvers.

Readers of my books and articles often assume that I carve very traditionally, using only carving tools, and never use sandpaper. But this is a reading based only on what is presented for publication; in fact I choose from a wider range of approaches and work in more and different ways than is readily apparent. It all depends on what I want to achieve.

I make the point several times in this book that it is *having the choice* of techniques which is important – having the freedom to create as close to your intent as you can, rather than settling for whatever you can manage by default. So I encourage learning: practise and explore, and try not to become fixed in your (or my) ways.

This project arose from my having a vigorous idea along with a particular approach to realize it. It demonstrates a close interaction between the three elements of woodcarving.

DESIGN

THE IDEA

We look up to see a struggling man, twisting in the bright, radiant light of the sun; colours, gold, warmth; a vulnerable body, exposed, head turned away; golden hair dazzling in the eye of heaven – these were some of the thoughts behind the image of the carving (Fig 7.1).

The actual positioning of the figure was not fully worked out until I had the piece of wood. I took

Fig 7.1 *The carving viewed from its intended angle. Making the legs smaller causes them to appear normal-sized in relation to the rest of the body when viewed from below*

accurate measurements of a piece nearest to what I had in mind and started rough sketching. Balancing and juggling my available wood with what I wanted to achieve, the shape of the figure emerged.

70

I was interested in getting a sense of energy and focus. Energy arises in the design with the dynamic use of 'lines of force' around the figure, passing out into space beyond; and with the horn-like feathers, cutting a second rhythm of lines through the first. Focus comes with the unifying of head and sun – this is the centre of the action, the point from which the figure of Ikarus seems to hang.

PERSPECTIVE

The trickiest problem in the design was what to do about the perspective. I wanted Ikarus to hang high up, in a stairwell, to be viewed by looking upward. In this way I am making the viewer participate in the story, looking up to see Ikarus fall.

The viewpoint from which a carving is to be seen – particularly in the case of relief carvings – is a very important early consideration. It is something not taken into account often enough by beginners, who, to be fair, have rather enough to think about already.

A relief carving has only one 'correct' viewpoint, where the carver wants the viewer to stand for best effect. The structure and perspective of the carving, including the relative sizes of parts, will depend on this viewpoint (see *Relief Carving in Wood*, page 40). In more practical terms, the viewpoint affects the extent of any undercutting and where it takes place. In this carving there is no undercutting, but the viewpoint was intended to be more 'acute' than the usual 'straight on'.

When the viewer looks from below at a relief carving, at such an acute angle, a lot of distortion takes place, in addition to that normally inherent in relief work. In this particular case the legs would appear a *lot* larger because they are nearer the viewer – and quite close up – and the arms would appear smaller because they are farther away.

I didn't fully appreciate this point when I made my working drawing. It was only when I was carving, with the advantage of the true perspective given me by the tilting bench, that I realized that, in order for the relief figure to appear correctly proportioned from the acute angle below, I was compensating with another distortion: reducing the leg size.

Fig 7.2 shows the final carving looked at straight on, and you can see that the legs look somewhat small. View the carving from below (Fig 7.1), and you will see the proportions corrected. A famous example of deliberate distortion of perspective appears in Holbein's painting *The Ambassadors* (but for entirely different reasons). There is a whole new style here for an innovative carver to explore!

Fig 7.2 *The finished carving looked at straight on. From this viewpoint the legs appear proportionately too small, but the distortion is corrected when the carving is seen from below, as intended (compare Fig 7.1)*

TEXTURE

An aspect of this carving which differentiates it from others in this book is my concern with making more use of the possibilities of surface texture. I created texture both in the grooves forming the circular 'rays' and in the feathers themselves by using burrs and cutters on a high-speed flexible shaft. Examining the surface close-up is almost like looking at abstract painting (Figs 7.3 and 7.4).

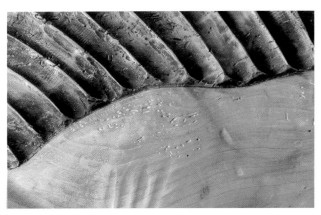

Fig 7.3 A close-up of Ikarus' body and the 'rays' gives the impression of a lunar landscape

Fig 7.4 The scoring marks left by a coarse rotary burr are clearly seen in the feather textures. Flexible-shaft machines are great for texturing and can be used almost like paintbrushes

I wanted contrast within the piece between the strong lines and texturing of wings and background and the smoothness of the body itself, emphasizing its nakedness. To this end I sanded the body; but I quite deliberately chose not to sand to an eggshell surface, but rather allow scratches of heavier grit to remain, almost as light 'doodling' marks. Again this is an exercise in choice: I am quite happy, and able, to render a surface immaculately smooth, and can therefore freely choose not to.

DRAWING

I based my drawing (Fig 7.5) closely on the shape of the available board, starting with a scale outline of the material and making many rough sketches. From these I worked up a final version which I transferred to the board, enlarging it to fit using the 'square-to-square' method. Although I had made a drawing, I saw this as just a working basis for the carving and not a blueprint to be slavishly followed; if nothing else, I did not know what the wood would reveal once I started cutting into it.

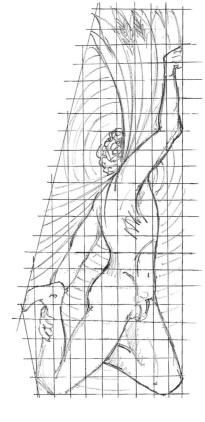

Fig 7.5 This is my working sketch of Ikarus, showing how the figure fits the contours of the board; I drew gridlines over it to scale so that I could transfer the drawing to the wood

WOOD

Sometimes one has an idea and chooses exactly the wood to fit. Sometimes it's the other way around: you have the wood and are looking for what you can do with it. In this case there was something of both approaches. I felt the widening of the board at the bottom could be used to enhance the effect of falling, drop-like. Then again, I fitted my design to this shape, and if the wood had had a different outline, the figure would have been different – perhaps the leg on the left would not have been held, or would have been held differently.

A natural elm board of this shape was what I had: always a warm-looking wood, often with softly wild grain, and easy to work if treated correctly (particularly if using the slicing cut – see Clean Cutting on page 68).

There was quite a lot of woodworm in the board (elm being prone to it), particularly in the relatively sappier edges. Because I knew that one interest for me in this carving was texture, I just ignored it!

HOLDING

I held the wood vertically on the tilting bench (see pages 16–19) with a carver's screw, leaning the work back so I could work from more or less the final viewpoint.

CARVING

The technique is similar to that of other relief carvings in this book – for example Dürer's Hands (Chapter 3) and Padmasambhava (Chapter 6): the surrounding background is reduced first, allowing the subject to stand proud, then the subject itself shaped and modelled. The background in this case appears a lot deeper than it is because of the deep trenches circling around.

TOOLS

I used conventional carving tools for the main roughing out and shaping. A router helped recess the area between the legs and between the ends of

the feathers. Later I brought in a flexible-shaft machine with a rotary burr and sanding drums for the modelling, and to texture and finish the surface.

In order to draw reasonably accurate circles I made a large adjustable trammel compass from bits of scrap wood; I used this continually to check the run of the grooves making up the rays.

CARVING

Start by running a V-tool along the drawing lines, getting a feel for them, and for the form as a whole (Fig 7.6). Next, large gouges are used to waste away the background, parts of which I allowed to rise from the figure to the surface at the edge of the board (Figs 7.7 and 7.8).

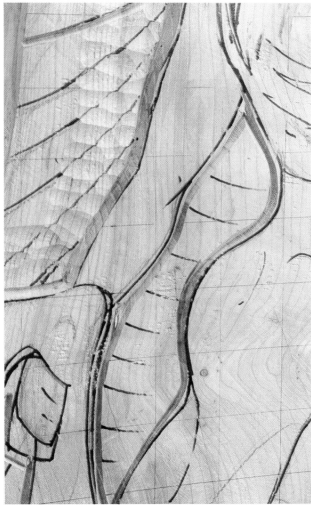

Fig 7.6 *A heavy lining in with the V-tool serves to protect the subject while the background is removed with large gouges*

Once the levels have been established, turn to the feathers and the circular rays, drawing them in first, then cutting them away. In the case of the rays it is particularly important to work with the grain to avoid breaking off the ridges between grooves; this meant taking either side of the groove in opposite directions (Fig 7.9). At the same time some of the figure can be roughed in (Fig 7.10).

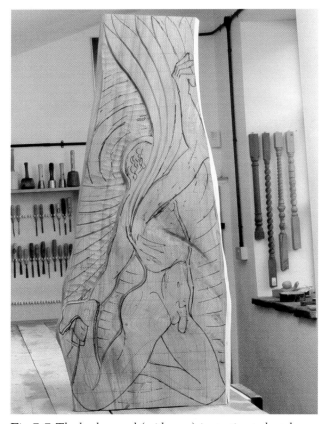

Fig 7.7 *The background (with rays) is starting to be taken lower than the wings*

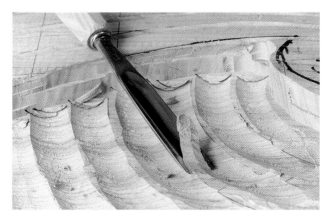

Fig 7.9 *Cutting the 'rays' in the background: here the ridge between two rays is being created by cutting with the grain along one side of the hollow. To work with the grain on the opposite side of the ray requires the gouge to cut in the reverse direction*

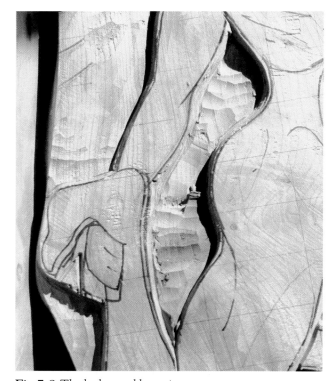

Fig 7.8 *The body roughly set in*

Fig 7.10 *Most of the background 'rays' have been cut, and bosting in of the legs has begun*

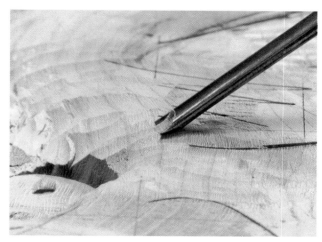

Figs 7.11 *The start of the cut*

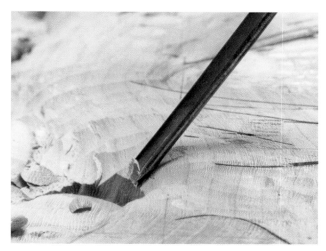

Fig 7.12 *Lifting the handle so the tool follows the curvature of the edge*

Fig 7.13 *At the end of its movement the tool is cutting vertically down towards the ground. Throughout the cut you are following the form you want, rather than just chamfering off edges*

Carving the figure itself proceeds as described in Notes on the Carving Process on page 24: main shapes first, then subsidiary ones, with detailing last.

One important point here: the best way to model a form is to use carving tools directly and three-dimensionally. *This means visualizing the form beneath and running your cuts on this imaginary surface.* For example, Figs 7.11–7.13 show the carving tool swinging around and into the hollow of the ground beneath. There is no series of flat planes – aim straightaway for the curved surface you want and which you try to 'see' beneath the cutting edge.

Hair can be carved mainly with the V-tool and skew chisel once the overall shape of the head has been established.

There comes a point when the edge of the figure has to be cleaned up to the rays (Fig 7.14); this is done by setting in with a skew chisel, into the depth of each groove.

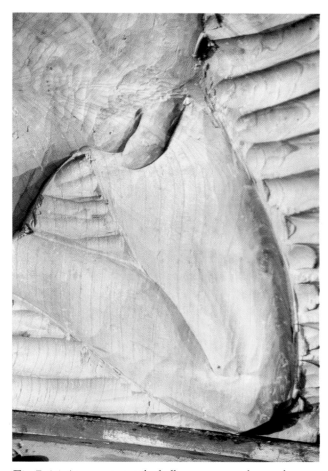

Fig 7.14 *At some point the hollow rays must be neatly cleaned up to the body*

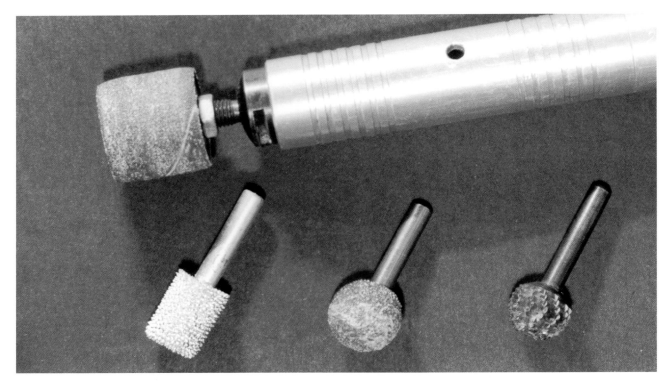

Fig 7.15 The Foredom high-speed flexible-shaft handpiece fitted with a rotary sanding drum (also shown are burrs with high-speed steel, tungsten carbide grit and sintered tungsten carbide teeth)

I encountered no special problems with this piece, except that the area of the wood which was most affected by the woodworm was crumbly – but nothing that gentle slicing cuts couldn't cope with. There are wood strengtheners on the market, intended for treating wood before painting, which can be used to reinforce crumbly wood.

When I had gone as far as possible with carving tools I turned to the flexible-shaft machine with a coarse 25mm (1in) sanding drum (Fig 7.15) to smooth over the surface for sanding by hand. More importantly, I used the edge of the drum to texture the feathers and to refine and texture the grooves and 'rays' (Fig 7.16).

The body is finally sanded to the required finish (see Smooth Surfaces on page 78).

Fig 7.16 Detail of head and shoulders, showing the texturing produced by the edge of a sanding drum used in a flexible-shaft machine

USING A HIGH-SPEED FLEXIBLE-SHAFT MACHINE

Some details of these tools, including safety advice, were given in *Woodcarving Tools, Materials & Equipment*, pages 227–8. They are versatile, taking a wide range of collets, cutters, burrs and sanding drums, and fairly straightforward to use. I would like to emphasize a few points:

Fast power tools, especially when used to sand or cut finely, generate very fine dust which often hangs in the air for hours after you've finished work and taken off any inhalation protection. Sufficient quantities of this dust can be a fire hazard, as it ignites easily above certain concentrations and, when settled, will conduct fire to other parts of the workshop.

Because the cutting action is controlled by pulling the handpiece *towards* the user – against the rotation of the sanding drum – dust and particles are mostly thrown in the user's direction. Particles of dust are easily inhaled, and simple face masks are almost totally ineffective against particles below a certain size. Larger particles, broken cutters, etc. will also head towards the face and eyes.

It just isn't worth the risk of either bronchial or lung damage or diseases, or injury to the eyes. A miserable end to a carving career!

Except for the smallest amount of occasional work, I never use the high-speed shaft in the workshop at all. I take the workpiece outside into the fresh air and even then still wear a fan-driven dust helmet. But this is in keeping with my carving style. If you are planning to make extensive use of these devices then you *must*, as part of the package (and the overall cost):

- Have a local dust collection system, ducting the air away from the workplace, and keep this system maintained (empty it regularly, use a good filter, etc.).

- Have an ambient air filter cleaning the room between sessions.

- Use a good face mask at least, better still a full-face, fan-operated helmet.

- Protect eyes – prescription glasses are not enough. If you wear a full helmet then you protect your eyes and face at the same time.

- Keep the work area clean by using, say, an industrial vacuum cleaner.

FINISHING

My first priority was to brush woodworm treatment fluid all over the board, wearing eye and hand protection and allowing the wood to dry in a well-ventilated room.

A blue water-based stain was applied to the background, and a red one to the hair and feathers; then high points were rubbed back to natural wood. Gilt wax was lightly and selectively applied over these stained parts to get the effect I wanted.

The figure of Ikarus was left with only a waxed finish. I used thin wax in several coats, rubbing in subsequent coats with nylon scouring pads and finally burnishing with a soft cloth.

CONCLUSION

This was a carving I greatly enjoyed, as the design, the materials and my approach seemed less constraining and allowed me to be more impulsive than is often the case. Ikarus contrasts nicely with the relief-carved Shirt of Chapter 8, which is a highly formal approach: the design is in trompe-l'œil and not metaphorical; the wood is subservient to the design; colour and other effects are absent; and everything is finished with cutting edges.

But this is one thing I love about woodcarving: the possibility of endless variety.

SECTION F

SMOOTH SURFACES

BEAUTIFUL EGGS AND BOILED SWEETS

With good toolwork, a clean, lightly textured smooth surface is not only possible but straightforward to produce. Such a surface, if correctly executed, has a distinctive lustre, a soft brightness; the handwork is immediately apparent, is capable of more expression – 'meaning', even – and more variety than a sanded surface; and the result is very individual to the carver.

Sometimes a *very* smooth surface is required – to bring out the grain of the wood, to provide a contrast with tooled areas, to satisfy the needs of the design, or maybe just to suit the style or inclination of the carver. In the right place, such smooth surfaces can look incredibly beautiful and add much to a carving.

I see finishing with a sanded surface as a *personal* choice of the carver, and not a moral one of 'right' or 'wrong'. However, in my experience, the sad truth is that many carvers actually know they sand as a 'quick' way of finishing something off, as a means of making poor work look presentable, or because they don't have the tool skills to do anything else.

When poorly or inappropriately done, the danger is that a sanded carving can look as though it has been sucked, rather like a boiled sweet, blending together all the changes of plane which are so characteristic of carving. And compared with surfaces well finished from the cutting edge, dead smooth ones can look dead indeed – or hard, like eggshell. Furthermore, sanded carvings all tend to look similar.

Sanding to an immaculate surface involves much harder work than carving, and, if done properly, is not the easy option many beginners think: it can be mind-numbingly tedious, and tough on the fingers and lungs. Here are some brief guidelines:

- *Study* your sandpaper: understand 'open' and 'closed' grits, and what works best for which wood; what the grade numbering system means; and what uses the different types of abrasive are suitable for.

- Carve, and then scrape, as close to the final surface as possible. In this way you cut down the amount of sanding needed, and you can start with a finer grit.

- Pay attention to edges and changes of plane, making sure these are preserved.

- Most students are too hasty – be patient! Work through the grits, without skipping any, *removing completely the scratches left by the previous paper before moving on*.

- Use the coarser grits across the grain for fast waste removal, but finish *with* the grain. As the grits get finer, work more *with* the grain so as not to leave scratches. Damp the wood and let it dry between sessions, to raise the grain.

- Wire wool snags in some woods, leaving particles embedded and making the surface look dirty. This can be disastrous in the case of oak and other woods which react with iron.

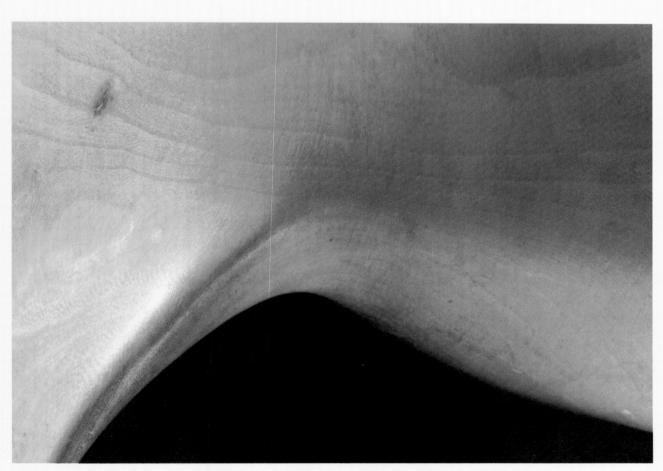

A detail from a large sculpture of a snail shell. How could this form be anything other than smooth?

CHAPTER 8

SHIRT

This interesting commission came from clients whose work seemed to give rise to endless numbers of shirts hanging in their flat, either drying or ready for ironing. Having suffered the humour of their friends for some while, they decided a wooden shirt might help turn the tables a little (Fig 8.1).

I hoped the viewer might have the urge to straighten the shirt on its hanger, only to find that it was a woodcarving after all. For added possibilities, I hollowed the pocket to hold assorted objects such as comb, mouse, etc., as the clients saw fit.

Realism came from deep undercutting, adding buttons made from horn, sanding the hanger and staining it to make it clearly distinct, and from the finely tooled surface. This painstaking finish left by the carving tools perfectly captures the effect of soft cotton material. I have seen sanded versions of shirts and tablecloths, and I think this surface treatment is never wholly convincing – to my mind, it gives a hard, 'eggshell' appearance.

The main challenges in this carving were hiding the joins in the wood; simplifying the rucks and folds in the fabric (Fig 8.2); and carving the collar to give an impression of thinness while leaving it adequate strength.

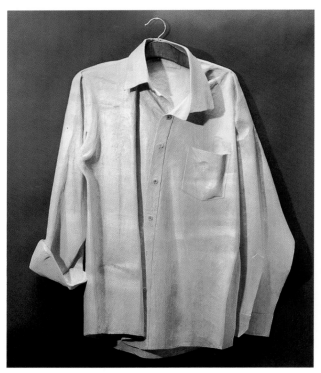

Fig 8.1 *The finished shirt, in sycamore, actually hangs from a keyhole plate at the back of the 'hanger' wood, rather than from the real hook fitted to the hanger*

DESIGN

The carving is full size and closely based on an actual shirt. I wanted the initial impression to be that of a real garment, hanging casually askew.

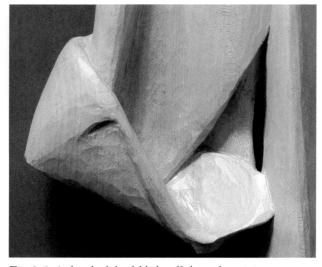

Fig 8.2 *A detail of the folded cuff shows how it is necessary to stylize, to simplify the form*

MODEL

A model to work from is essential, if the carving is to fool anyone – so first catch your shirt. Arrange it on a suitable hanger, giving depth and interest with a folded cuff, a missing button and so on.

Your model must remain a constant shape while you are working, so you can take measurements from it. I stiffened the fabric with Unibond adhesive, diluted with 15 parts water, sprayed from a gardening diffuser (Fig 8.3). I packed paper into the pocket to keep it open. When dry, I tacked the sleeves to the body of the shirt with hot-melt glue.

Fig 8.3 *The 'model' shirt, sprayed with fixative and hanging up to dry*

DRAWING

A drawing (Fig 8.4) will help you simplify what is actually quite a complex form. You can cut this drawing into templates for measuring and assembling the wood, and for drawing out the shirt for the bandsaw.

Draw round the outline of the shirt on to a large piece of paper with pencil or felt-tip pen (Fig 8.5).

For the internal details such as main seams and buttonholes, prick though the fabric into the paper with a fine awl held truly vertical (Fig 8.6). Firm up the drawing by checking measurements against the original shirt (Fig 8.7).

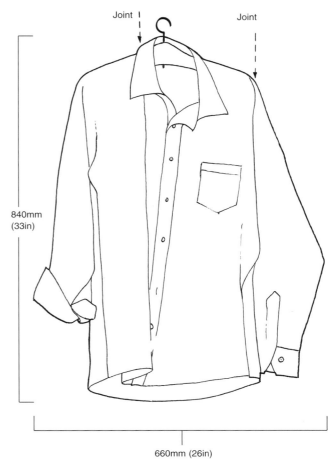

840mm (33in)

660mm (26in)

Wood thickness 75mm (3in)

Fig 8.4 *A working drawing will allow you to calculate what wood you need and where best to put joints, and to simplify what is actually quite a complicated sculptural form*

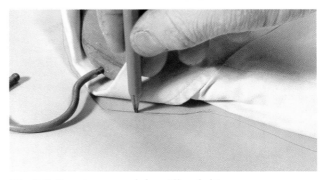

Fig 8.5 *Drawing around the stiffened shirt on to paper to produce a working drawing*

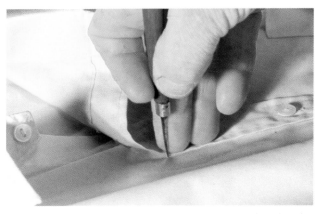

Fig 8.6 *Pricking through internal details and landmarks: the awl must be held accurately vertical*

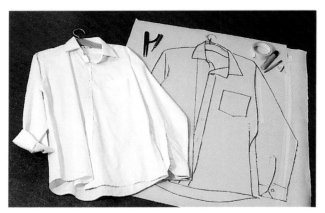

Fig 8.7 *The stiffened 'model' shirt next to the finished working drawing*

WOOD

I used air-dried European sycamore with straight, tight grain and no knots to give a pale off-white colour. It tends to 'stick' to the carving tools and is not a wood I normally choose to carve; however, the final colour and figure were perfect. Lime or maple might be alternatives.

The height of the carving was 840mm (33in) and the width 660mm (26in), with a thickness of 75mm (3in). The grain direction is vertical. *Be sure to use a thick enough piece of wood, otherwise your carving will look flat and unconvincing.*

JOINING

I was unable to find a single slab of wood this size, so I glued up three pieces, along the lines shown in the drawing, which enables the joints to be successfully

hidden. Good butt joints without dowels are quite adequate (Fig 8.8).

If you glue up, remember: aim for immaculate, fine joints, hide the glue lines in the folds or seams, and match the figure as closely as possible. In this way the joints will be nearly invisible. In my shirt the only place where a joint is visible is where one runs across the collar (Fig 8.9), but because I followed these criteria the joint is not obtrusive.

Clean up the back first – I used a belt sander – and bandsaw the wood to the outline of the shirt.

Fig 8.8 *Gluing up: tight, immaculate butt joints (no dowels), with matched grain and joints which will be hidden in the folds of the material, will give an almost invisible result.*

Fig 8.9 *Detail of the collar. A slight change of grain shows the join in the collar on the left of the picture. The rest of the join goes down the fold and is practically invisible*

HOLDING

I carved the shirt almost vertically, held on the tilting bench (see pages 16–19) with a Stubai woodcarver's screw. The screw must be fixed *where maximum thickness will remain in the carving*, so some calculation is needed. The screw may be well off centre – as was mine – but should still hold the work more than competently. The only drawback to this method is the hole, which will eventually need a plug of the same wood. However, I found this the most convenient way to clamp the work once shaping was well under way.

CARVING

Although I am giving details of a specific shirt here, I expect that everyone attempting this project will arrange the subject differently; so I will only give the broad outlines of my approach and guidelines on the stages, the techniques and some of the problems you might encounter.

Study your starting block of wood well before you do anything else. The forms are quite complicated and you can't put in every crease and wrinkle; we need to prioritize. Look for:

- **The main flowing lines**: these you should know from your drawing, but observe how they must move three-dimensionally.

- **How the folds hang**: how does the shape at the shoulders relate to the hanger underneath? Look for points of tension (from which the shirt hangs) and relaxation (into the folds).

- **Areas of hardness** (such as the collar and hanger) and softness (pocket and folds) – which require different surface tooling.

- **High points** from which wood will hardly be removed at all.

- **Useful reference points** such as the tips of the collar, the centre of the hanger, and the buttons.

- **Three-dimensionality**: there is a lot of wood to remove; in some parts the shirt is only 6mm (¼in) thick from the back. You must make full use of the depth to give the correct effect.

ROUGHING OUT

Bandsaw the shirt outline. Mark in the high points with red chalk; these are *areas to leave*; work inwards from them.

Bore the 3mm (⅛in) holes to take the button spigots (Fig 8.10). These spigot holes are of great help when measuring, once the drawn lines have been carved away. You *could* carve the buttons in, but shirt buttons are normally made from a contrasting material and it adds greatly to the realism if you turn these (with a spigot) or carve them separately.

You now have several reference points to measure and work from:

1   the outline,

2   the marked high points,

3   the button spigot holes,

4   the shirt model,

5   your drawing.

Fig 8.10 *The button spigot holes are very useful reference points and were bored in first*

To rough out the form I used an Arbortech (Fig 8.11) and a large gouge, swapping between the two. Seek the main masses, lines and points from which the lines flow so that bosting in follows smoothly.

You should not make any hard edges at this stage, even though you are creating depth at various places. The work should look 'out of focus' and soft when you have finished, rather than a series of hard planes (Fig 8.12).

At some point the shape and speed of the Arbortech become too dominant in the carving process, and carving then continues with large gouges only, so moving into the next stage.

BOSTING IN

Now you can begin refining the main masses of the shirt, pushing away the wood as you follow the planes into the depths and keeping the cutting as clean as possible (Fig 8.13). Always treat the carving as a whole – don't finish off one part while other parts are still rough. Resist the temptation to put in seams or details; these will naturally fall into place as the shapes are refined.

Fig 8.11 Primary roughing out with the Arbortech. High spots have been marked out in red as 'no-go areas'. Note the holes where the shirt buttons will go. I carved the shirt vertically on the tilting bench (see pages 16–19), with the model to hand for reference

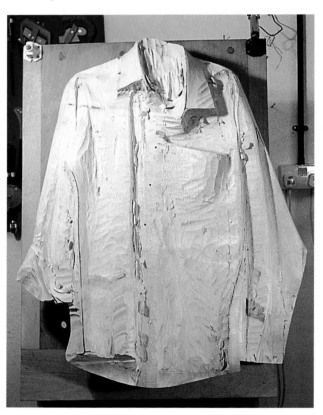

Fig 8.13 After the Arbortech come the large gouges: some of the main forms of the shirt are now appearing, and the collar surface has been placed

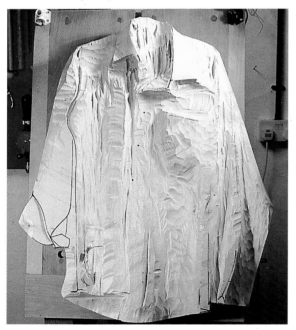

Fig 8.12 This is as far as I went with the Arbortech. An 'unfocused' effect, lacking hard edges, is appropriate at this stage

I found it very useful to place the plane of the collar quite accurately early on, following it round to the back of the shirt. As a general rule, *do not undercut anything* (such as the collar) *until you are really sure of the surface position*. Allow the undercutting to arise from passing round the form, rather than being something which is 'applied'.

Use as large gouges as possible (Figs 8.14 and 8.15). Both a block plane and a (sharp!) spokeshave are helpful for the arms and principal folds, and a fine rasp is useful on the collar.

As you refine the shapes you will need to keep referring to the model, simplifying where necessary and measuring with dividers from established reference points such as the tips of the collars or the button holes. Eventually you will find the bosting-in stage has quietly merged with subsequent modelling.

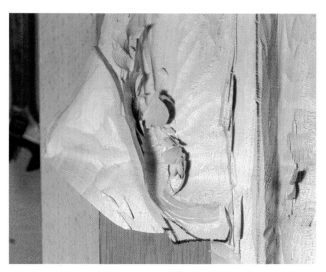

Fig 8.14 *Beginning to get depth in the right cuff, using a large gouge*

Fig 8.15 *On the left cuff, a large flattish gouge keeps the defining of planes simple. Note the pencil lines and other reference marks on the wood*

MODELLING

The shirt should now be taking shape (Fig 8.16), and you can turn your attention to the hanger inside the collar, one of the trickier bits of the carving.

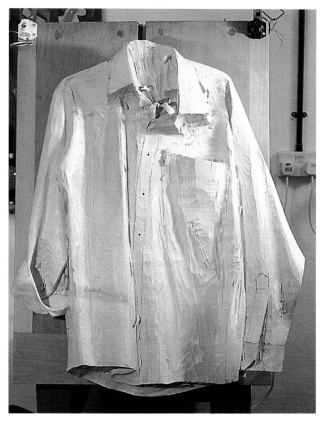

Fig 8.16 *After further work with gouges, some of the folds are becoming more defined. A block plane was used on the long surfaces of the arms*

COLLAR

A warning: when the top part of the collar (above and behind the metal hook) has been chamfered from the back, it will end up about 3mm (⅛in) thick. The grain is also short here, and consequently this part of the carving is the weakest and most vulnerable. So *you must not lever on it* with the carving tools while cutting within: any pressure here will break the wood.

Establish the centre of the flat plane of the hanger first, at the correct depth, by way of a datum. Mark in the centre where the metal hook will go. Use shortbent gouges to work right and left, under and into the shoulders as far as you can (Fig 8.17).

Fig 8.17 *You will need shortbent (spoon-bit) gouges to work inside the collar. The area shaded in pencil is the start of the flat surface of the hanger*

Fig 8.18 *Further shortbent tools, especially a 60° V-tool, will help in excavating beneath the collar. It is important to give an impression of the hanger continuing beneath the collar and into the shoulders*

Fig 8.19 *The shirt is now starting to look something like the model: the main forms, lines and lower edges are in place, and there is a sense of depth*

You will need to visualize the line of the hanger inside the shirt as if it really does support the material at the shoulders. This is vital for creating the illusion of the shirt 'hanging'.

Draw in and carve the top edge of the hanger and the inside back of the collar next. It is from here onwards that especial care must be taken. Don't make the collar wood too thin. Lever against your thumb rather than the wood.

Draw and carve the lower edge of the hanger and reduce the flat (the inside back) of the shirt. The wood will be about 6mm (¼in) thick here. You can allow enough to carve the shirt label in low relief.

Extend the carving inside the collar to each side and begin to undercut (Figs 8.18 and 8.19). You will find backbent tools useful here. Try to work as cleanly as possible.

SURFACE

Now we return to the rest of the shirt. Up to this stage the carving should feel a little 'unfocused' or 'soft', but soon the final surfaces of the principal forms will start to be reached. You can now begin firming up or focusing: adding more definition to various parts, deepening creases, beginning to undercut, piercing through between arms and body, backing off the outer profile from behind to make the shirt appear thin (Fig 8.20). Always try to see the carving as a whole.

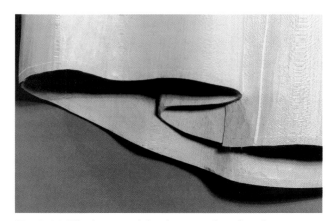

Fig 8.20 *The bottom of the shirt is nothing less than 'linenfold' and can be carved as such. Carve the surface folds first, then the ends*

Fig 8.22 *Two tools which enabled me to scoop out the pocket were made from a knife and a not-very-useful spare gouge*

DETAILING

The carving should look nearly there now (Fig 8.23) as we move into the last stages.

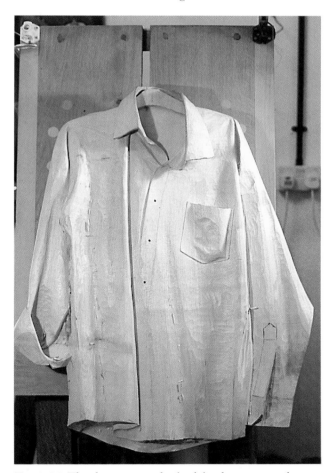

Fig 8.21 *Setting in true lines for the button seam – which is low relief – with masking tape. Note how this hard line cuts diagonally down to the left over a soft fold which runs down to the right. The inside collar and hanger are finished, but the outside of the collar is still to be carved*

SEAMS

I used masking tape to establish a line for the seams where the buttons will go (Fig 8.21). This band of material should be flat, to imply thicker material, contrasting with the more rounded thinner stuff next to it.

COLLAR AND POCKET

The material around the collar can now be shaped. The collar itself will need support: undercut it enough to make it appear thin, while leaving a gusset of wood for strength.

I needed two specially made hooked tools (Fig 8.22) to excavate the pocket, as my shortbents neither went deep enough nor worked *with* the grain (in other words, from the bottom of the pocket upwards to the edge). You can make these using information in my book *Woodcarving Tools, Materials & Equipment* (pages 229–51). Make the pocket deep enough to allow interesting objects (or parts of them) to peek out, and take care again not to lever against the weak edge.

Fig 8.23 *The shirt prior to the final finishing stage, when the surface will be smoothed over with flat gouges. The collar is finished; note the tension ruck in the fabric at the top button – selection of such details is one of the design challenges presented by this piece*

Work over the whole surface methodically with flat gouges, which must be as sharp as possible. Despite your best efforts, sycamore is an easy wood to get grubby, especially round the collar, so finish off and work away from clean areas. Clean up the junctions, true the lines and create a fine, lightly textured surface over all the carving before putting in final details.

When you think the carving is finished, change the lighting and look again – you will be surprised at what needs touching up. Then leave the carving covered for a while before returning with a fresh eye for a final check.

STITCHING

The sewing around the edges of the fabric can be implied by lightly scoring lines either with a knife or with a small scratch stock (Fig 8.24).

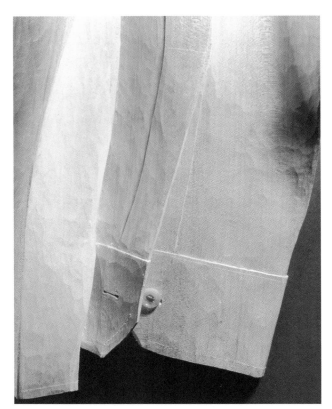

Fig 8.25 Detail of the long sleeve. It is important to get the correct sense of tension and relaxation in the material. The buttons are turned from cow horn, with a small spigot to insert into holes in the wood

HANGING

Sand the wood of the hanger to a smooth finish. I inserted a metal hook from a real (plastic) hanger into a hole bored carefully from above (Fig 8.26). The carving actually hangs from a brass keyhole plate at the back, rather than this wire hook – I never really trusted the latter. When the shirt is placed in its final position, a nail is driven into the wall beneath the hook to give the illusion that it hangs conventionally.

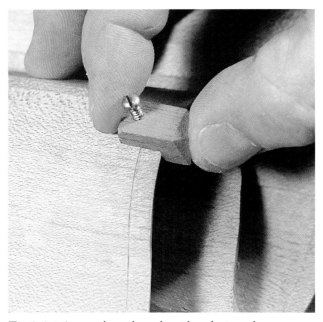

Fig 8.24 A scratch stock made with a sharpened screw scores the wood to imitate lines of stitching

BUTTONS

Turn or carve the buttons; I used some old cow horn which had been given me (Fig 8.25). Bone from a butcher's is a suitable substitute, or you could use a contrasting type of wood. You can also buy artificial ivory from specialist craft suppliers.

FINISH

The hanger was treated with a dark oak gloss varnish for contrast (Fig 8.27). The buttons were made shiny with clear gloss varnish, also for contrast. The wood of the shirt was sealed with clear shellac and given several coats of thin beeswax for a light sheen.

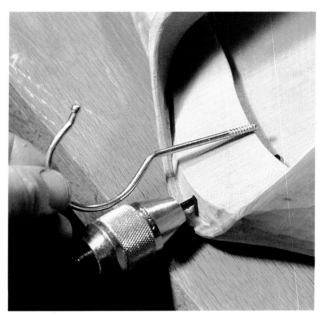

Fig 8.26 *The hanger hook came from a real plastic hanger and will simply push through the hole prepared for it. The shirt is actually suspended from the wall by a fixing at the back*

CONCLUSION

The greatest compliment I have had for this carving was: 'How did you get the hanger in there?' – which to me means the carving was successful!

Fig 8.27 *Detail of the hanger – made in one piece with the shirt – and metal hook. The most vulnerable part is the thin section of the collar with short grain to the right of the metal hook. A label has been carved in low relief and the lightly tooled surface, which gives an effect of fabric-like softness, is clearly visible*

CLEAN WORK

HABITS IN ACTION

It doesn't take long for carving students to find out how effortlessly bare wood fibres attract dirt and absorb grease.

Woodcarvings, at all stages, can look dirty and grubby very easily. Grime is impossible to remove without recutting or sanding – which must extend over the whole area to avoid blotchiness. Grime affects stains and finishes; it dulls the shine of the finished work.

Here are some guidelines to prevent your carvings suffering in this way. The real trick is to cultivate habits of clean working, preventing the problem in the first place.

CLEAN HANDS

Your hands will readily pick up dirt and transfer it to the workpiece. Watch out for:

- oil from sharpening stones,

- grease from strops,

- sweat and natural oils on the hands,

- dirt on the bench or work surface;

- rubbing drawn pencil lines on the carving with the heel of your hand;

- wiping your hands on dirty trousers, overalls or aprons.

Wash your hands regularly with warm water and soap. If there is no sink to hand, an arrangement of kettle, camping water-barrel and bowl will serve well. Use felt-tip pens for drawing on carvings, or mask pencil lines with tape (see Fig 6.6 on page 63).

Cotton gardening gloves will protect the wood against perspiration from the hands.

CLEAN TOOLS

Wipe them after using oil or the strop; they will also pick up dirt from a grubby bench if just left unused for a long time. Have a kitchen roll hanging to hand. Put your tools away when you have finished with them.

CLEAN BENCH

'Clear the decks for action!' and generally keep the bench clean of wood chips, dust and old rags. Wipe it with a damp cloth occasionally.

CLEAN WORKSHOP

Wood shavings and chips, dust and old rags collect and create dirt. Clean up regularly. An (industrial power) vacuum cleaner is far better than brushes, which put dirt into the air to settle again later.

CLEAN WORK

Cover your work between sessions, with either a clean plastic bag or a cloth. In the final stages – where you are coming to a final surface – rest your hands on a piece of clean cloth or kitchen paper, or wear cotton gloves.

Door pediment (tympanum) with acanthus leaf and volute in oak; height of carving 380mm (15in). The whole carving, including the ground, has been left from the chisel. Since this carving will be finished only with a clear sealer, and will be displayed in full view of the public, it must leave the workshop looking its best – clean and tidy!

CHAPTER 9

LEAPING FROG

The focus of this book is to demonstrate that in any woodcarving there is a working together, a co-operation, of three elements or factors: the **design** (the vision, translated into something of interest to the viewer); the **technique** (the sharpness of the tools and the carver's ability to use them); and the **material**, the wood (making the best use of its properties, such as strength).

In this carving of a frog (Figs 9.1–9.3), the element which holds the work together and supports the design is the wood. It is in using the grain that the challenge of this fairly advanced piece of carving lies. The design requires the grain of the wood to give hidden strength to what appears to be a fragile piece of work.

If you want to attempt this or a similar carving, it is vital that your tools are very sharp indeed: as the work becomes more fragile, sharp cutting edges will minimize pressure on the weaker parts of the carving. Unless you use sandpaper, the quality of the surface finish will be the direct result of your cutting edges. Make sure the bevels are flat and no scratch marks trail in the cut facets.

Fig 9.1 *The finished carving: left side view. From this viewpoint the leaping frog does not appear to be attached to the base at all*

Fig 9.2 *Front view*

Fig 9.3 *View from the right-hand side*

DESIGN

THE IDEA

A moment of drama: a frog leaps from its lily pad to snatch a passing fly with its tongue. The leaf buckles as the powerful back legs push the frog into the air.

The lily pad is first and foremost a device to support the frog in a believable way as it takes to the air; there must be many ways to achieve this aim. I wanted the frog to touch the leaf as little as possible – in fact, it touches with only one knee and foot. The key problem in the design was how to get strength into the legs, arms, tongue and fly.

The answer was to run the grain along both legs, up through the tongue and into the wings of the fly, so all these elements are supported by the long wood fibres. The free leg is at a different angle from the supporting one, but still contains a lot of diagonally placed fibres. The frog's arms are held in to its sides, which keeps them strong. The fly is skewed in position so as to get the longest grain possible in the wings. The weakest parts are the frog's fingers, which I therefore made a little stubbier than they would be in real life.

In this way, the wood works intimately with the design. The free leg of the frog, like the wings of the fly, remains flexible, but resists an edge firmly enough to be cut cleanly by the sharp tools, somewhat after the fashion of the butterfly carving of Chapter 12. The finished piece is still a delicate piece of woodcarving, and needs to be carefully handled, but it is by no means as fragile as it looks.

I think that in retrospect I would have made the design a little different. For example, I would have tucked the arms back along the body (which is more commonly what happens when a frog jumps); poked the tongue out a lot further; carved a more interesting fly separately (instead of fixating on the 'look, one piece' angle); and tried a different shape to the leaf. You may like to consider these points if you are thinking about tackling this project.

DRAWING AND MODEL

I made preliminary sketches from photographs and anatomy books, and used these as a basis for a Plasticine model (see Modelling on pages 46–7). There is not space to go into frog anatomy here, but do remember that *research is never wasted*. If you intend to have a go at this carving, I would strongly advise you to start by drawing frogs and making a clay or Plasticine model too.

The model helped me pin down the image and give me a feel for the form and anatomy of the subject. It also allowed me to measure fairly accurately for material, and helped me solve problems such as strength early on. It was from this model that I made a full-size working drawing (Figs 9.4 and 9.5).

WOOD

I chose tight, clean limewood for the carving. The frog is one with the central part of the leaf, and two separate pieces make the sides of the leaf. I chose to carve the central piece, down to the frog's knees, before attaching the side parts. This gave me easier access to the underside of the frog without excess wood getting in the way.

All three pieces were cut from a block of lime 14 x 14 x 3in (350 x 350 x 75mm), allowing the frog itself to be positioned on the diagonal. Cut out the main part so as to leave offcuts for the two smaller side pieces.

Get the best wood you can, avoiding sapwood: the quality of material is crucial to the strength of this carving. It is easier if you start with the limewood planed up.

HOLDING

You will see from the photographs that I changed the method of holding the carving after gluing up the leaves. I started with an adjustable vice to hold the central (frog) piece of wood. A bench vice would do as well, although being able to reposition carvings to get at a particular area more easily is a real advantage.

After adding the sides of the lily pad, I flattened off the underside of the carving with a belt sander and glued it to a piece of waste wood with newspaper in the joint. The waste wood was then held in another adjustable holding device (a Spencer Franklin

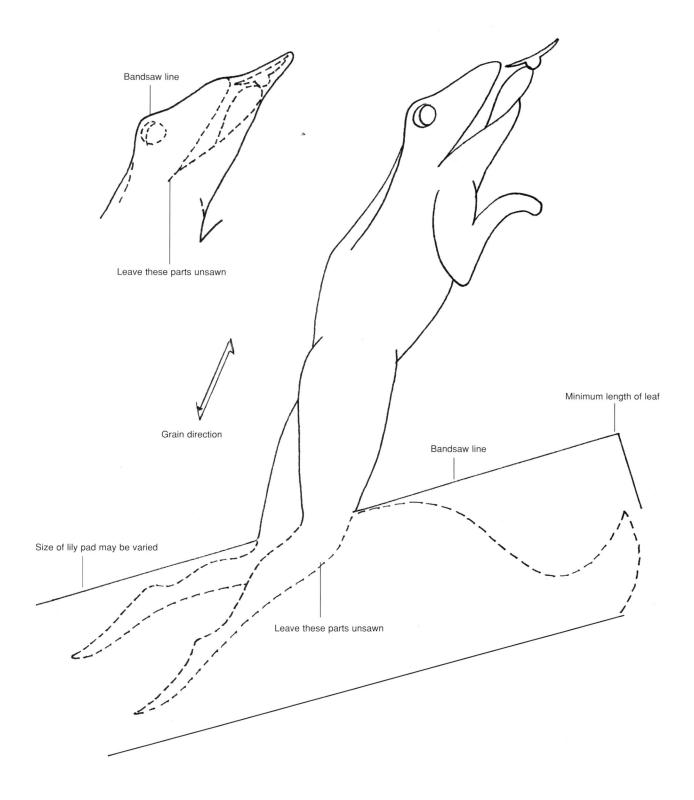

Bandsaw line

Leave these parts unsawn

Grain direction

Size of lily pad may be varied

Minimum length of leaf

Bandsaw line

Leave these parts unsawn

Fig 9.4 *Side view of the carving. Although the rough dimensions and shape of the lily pad are shown here, there is a lot of scope for variation, and I strongly advise you make a clay or Plasticine model to help you decide on the three-dimensional shape. You might also like to extend the tongue further*

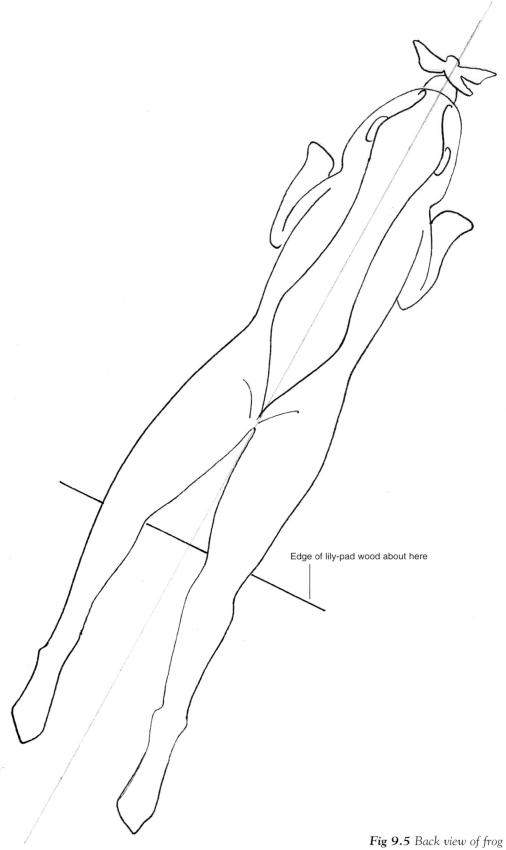

Edge of lily-pad wood about here

Fig 9.5 *Back view of frog*

Hydroclamp) for the second stage of carving and undercutting the leaf. To attach the waste wood, use PVA (white) glue, diluted by about a third with water. Brush it on to the clean, flat waste wood. Add a layer of non-glossy newsprint. Brush more glue on the base of the carving and clamp up the newspaper sandwich well, leaving to dry thoroughly before proceeding. A spatula will split the paper to release the finished carving.

CARVING

ROUGHING OUT

Great care must be taken to line up the side elevation drawing with the grain of the wood. Transfer the drawing with carbon paper and bandsaw the profile (Figs 9.6 and 9.7).

Although I had worked out where the lily pad was positioned below the frog, I left this part unsawn so as to give myself a degree of latitude in placing the legs and shaping the leaf. This is why so little of the leaf is shown in the drawings: I used the Plasticine model for reference instead.

Now draw the back view of the frog on to the wood (Fig 9.8). *Make sure it registers with the side view drawing.* A lot of the waste wood can be taken off with a coping saw (Fig 9.9); there is no way to get in with the bandsaw. Keep the coping saw vertical to the face of the wood. Now at last you are ready to start carving proper.

Fig 9.7 *Cutting the profile on the bandsaw. The drilled hole allows the workpiece to be rotated easily at this point*

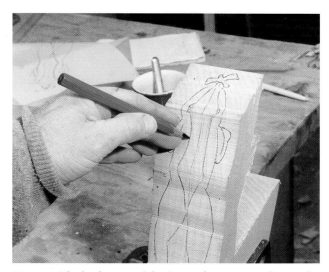

Fig 9.8 *The back view of the frog is drawn on to the wood*

Fig 9.6 *Transferring the drawing to the wood with carbon paper. Note how the grain is orientated along the frog. The straight baseline beneath the lily pad has been marked on the wood; the spare wood to the side will be used later to make up the width of the lily pad*

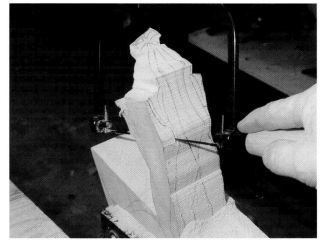

Fig 9.9 *Waste is removed with a coping saw. Note that plenty of wood has been left beneath*

CARVING THE CENTRE PIECE

It is worth noting that, out of the total time taken to produce the finished carving, at least a third was needed – in drawings, models, wood selection and bandsawing – to get to this stage.

The approach to carving this project differs a little from that described in Notes on the Carving Process on page 24. Because of the increasing fragility of the piece, you have to see yourself in the position of sitting on the limb of a tree, sawing off bits from the far end as you work your way towards the trunk. So, after an initial overall bosting in of the principal form (Fig 9.10), start at the 'fly and tongue' end and work your way down towards the feet, modelling and detailing a section at a time.

Remember: as a carving principle, *always cut the surface cleanly and leave it clean*. In this way you avoid having to go back tediously cleaning up torn grain at a later stage, when the carving is getting weaker.

FLY

As the fly takes shape you will need to support the wood with your fingers and use the carving tool with one hand (Figs 9.11 and 9.12). The fly is always the most vulnerable part of this carving, and you need to be continuously mindful of your actions to avoid breaking it off.

If you do have an accident and break the fly, see if you can glue the piece back – a clean break will often give an invisible join. Superglue is often perfect for such small repairs. Otherwise, you may choose to carve another fly separately – in which case you can probably make something far more interesting anyway, since you have freedom in the way you orientate the grain.

You will need to use small tools and hold your breath a lot to carve the fly. I think this was probably the trickiest part of the carving, so if you succeed here you should find the rest easier.

MOUTH

The fly and tongue lead naturally to the mouth, which is well undercut inside. A frog's tongue is a bit like a blob on a stalk, so there is plenty of room in the mouth.

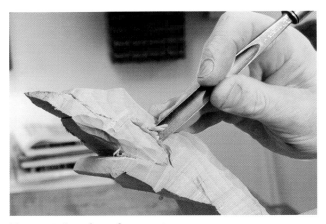

Fig 9.10 *Initial roughing out in progress*

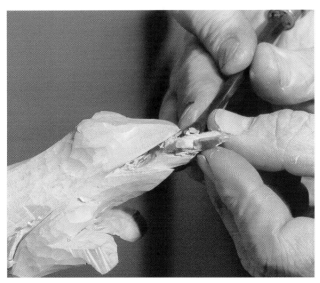

Fig 9.11 *Detailed carving starts with the fly, at the end farthest from the base*

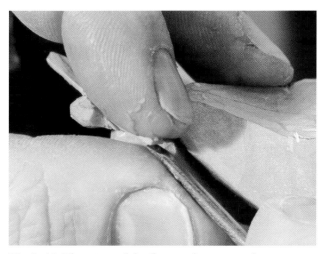

Fig 9.12 *The wings of the fly must be supported as you carve them*

EYES

I exaggerated the eye of the frog to give an alert, almost startled look, as it targets the fly. Do try and get a sense of the eyeball for what it is: a small ball pushing up the skin on the top of the frog's head (Figs 9.13–9.15). At all stages, the tool marks can be used to suggest anatomy: bone, tendons and skin quality. Fig 9.16 shows the head complete.

Fig 9.13 *Setting in the eye with a gouge of appropriate radius*

Fig 9.14 *Shaping the outer part of the eye surround*

Fig 9.15 *Working around the eye to shape the face. Finish off the farther parts of the frog first, before working down the body*

Fig 9.16 *Close-up of the completed head, tongue and fly. The roof of the mouth is well undercut and the nostrils are suggested*

SPINE AND ARMS

From the sides of the head you can now come down the frog's spine. The spine sets the dynamic of the carving. As the spine takes shape you can also work outwards to the arms, defining their position and removing wood from beneath to separate them from the body and each other (Fig 9.17). Move on from here to carve the front feet of the frog (Fig 9.18).

Fig 9.17 *Setting in the arms. The area from throat to chest is also worked on at this stage*

Fig 9.18 *Front toes being defined. The wood here is at its weakest, since the toes run across the grain, so great care is needed; a discreet amount of extra thickness may be left beneath for strength*

LEGS

From the arms, continue down the frog to the legs, finishing off the bottom of the spine. The legs themselves can be given a rough shaping, but there is no need to separate them yet.

LOWER LEGS AND BASE

JOINING

The next stage is to glue on the side pieces of the lily pad (Fig 9.19). The joints need to be immaculate right across – there is to be a lot of undercutting, which will greatly reduce the amount of actual joint surface. Make sure the grain direction matches exactly in all three pieces, and the glue lines are as small and neat as possible.

When dry, the rough outline of the lily pad can be bandsawn (Fig 9.20), and the workpiece glued to the waste wood with newspaper as described earlier (Fig 9.21).

Fig 9.19 Gluing up the side pieces. The grain is orientated in the same direction in all three pieces, and matched as well as possible

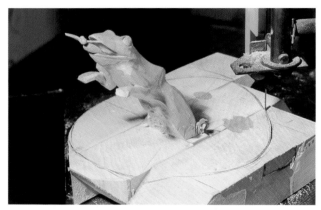

Fig 9.20 Bandsawing the lily-pad profile. The straight line on its surface indicates the axis of the leaf. The leaf can be any shape you want, as long as the finished work remains stable

Fig 9.21 Gluing the base block to a board (with newspaper in between) for the next stage of carving

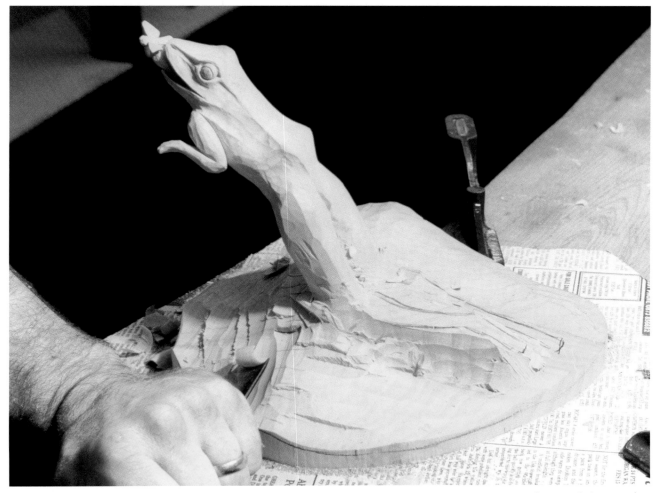

Fig 9.22 Bosting in the leaf shape and the position of the frog's legs. It is important to get an uncontrived, natural shape to the leaf, as if it had just buckled as the frog leapt

BOSTING IN AND MODELLING

Some of the heavy shaping of the leaf can be done with the work clamped to the bench (Fig 9.22), before mounting it on the adjustable clamp. It is at this point that the positions of both legs need to be set in and the shape of the lily pad arrived at. The lily pad can be further shaped at the same time as the shins and feet are carved. Use the full thickness of the wood to get a dynamic effect.

Shape the powerful thighs of the frog; as their form develops, allow the hole between them to emerge naturally.

It is advisable to leave some precautionary 'ties' (bits of wood joining a weak part to a strong part) between the shin of the free leg and the wood of the leaf below (Fig 9.23). This will enable you to work on the leg with added confidence. The ties need not

Fig 9.23 Defining the legs. Note the two 'ties' which support the farthest leg at this stage. When undercutting the near leg, remember that the frog is supported mainly by the grain of the wood which passes through the knee of this leg, so don't weaken it too much

Fig 9.24 *When the ties have been removed, one leg of the frog is completely free of the lily pad; the other is pierced beneath the shin. Both legs still have quite a lot of strength because of the grain direction*

Fig 9.25 *Texturing the leaf surface with a shallow gouge to imply ribs and veins*

be removed until the final stage when the leg is separated completely from the leaf, by which time it is at its weakest.

The opposite leg is undercut at the shin so that it touches the leaf lightly at only two points. Carve the main shape of the feet before defining the toes and the webbing between them.

At this point the frog is almost finished. If you have kept the cutting clean and the tool marks meaningful, there is little more to be done (Fig 9.24). The last job is the lily pad itself.

LILY PAD

The surface of the leaf is textured with marks from a shallow gouge, which radiate from an imaginary centre corresponding to where the stalk would be beneath (Fig 9.25). A tightly bent knuckle gouge is useful for the more difficult areas (Fig 9.26). Remember that you *can* cut *against* the grain using light cuts and a very sharp edge.

Fig 9.26 *To get at this part of the leaf, and cut cleanly with the grain, I use this home-bent knuckle gouge*

When the top surface of the lily pad is complete, it is time for vigorous undercutting (Fig 9.27). You need to leave enough wood, and in the right places, to make the piece stable, but otherwise try to get a thin appearance to the edges.

The finished carving is separated from the supporting waste wood with a spatula, inserted along the line of the newspaper. Clean up the undercutting with a gouge, then drag the underside of the base along a sheet of sandpaper to remove any residual newspaper.

Fig 9.27 *Undercutting the lily pad. Some waste can be removed with a drill first. The supporting board of waste wood may be cut into as necessary, and sawn away if it obstructs the carving*

Fig 9.28 *Brushing on thin wax to finish*

FINISHING

All the carving needs is a couple of coats of beeswax, applied and burnished with stiff artist's brushes, to seal and polish it (Fig 9.28).

CONCLUSION

I think this carving offers a very clear demonstration of the principle that, for a carving such as this to 'work' – to physically succeed – the three elements of design, tools and wood must come together nicely.

The fibres of the wood were orientated to give as much support as possible to the weaker elements of the subject. Any other orientation than the one I used, and the legs or the fly would be just too weak to survive either the carving process or subsequent life on the mantelpiece. The design also required a variety of tool techniques and the sharpest possible cutting edges. The carving also illustrates how ties can be used to offer temporary strength.

MISTAKES AND REPAIRS

FORESIGHT AND MAGIC

Mistakes and accidents arise from many causes:

- Not following the logical carving process, and removing wood where you will need it later (for example, by premature undercutting).

- Not taking into account the weaknesses or strengths of your material.

- Being heavy-handed, or levering with the blade rather than cutting.

- Using blunt tools, or not appreciating that the bevel of the tool is really just a refined wedge.

- Defects such as splits or knots, which develop unexpectedly even in seasoned wood.

Since we are human, and working in a material which is not wholly predictable, these things happen. The more experience and competence you have, the more concentration and foresight you bring to bear, the less often they occur. You will learn to use the strength of the wood in weak elements; build in supporting 'ties', even if these are cut away at the last moment; and find ways of handling the tools while supporting the work at the same time.

BREAKAGES

Small, neat breakages can be glued back on and recarved; they are usually invisible. Some pressure is needed; try masking tape or C-shaped clamps made from bedsprings, or wedge the part against some fixed object. Larger parts need very careful setting.

If the break is rough-fitting, it is better to resurface both parts and insert fresh wood to make up the width. Never use glue-and-sawdust mixtures as fillers unless the site is to be painted or hidden – this always looks unsightly and smacks of poor workmanship. Repair with wood instead.

SPLITS

Repair these with wedges, matched for grain direction and figuring, not with glue-and-sawdust fillers. Small cracks can be filled with colour-matched wax.

DEFECTS

On page 42 (Green Man 1) you will see a dead, rotten knot being replaced by a live one. On page 66 (Padmasambhava) a special insert called a 'Dutchman' is used. Both methods are effective and inconspicuous if used properly.

ABSENCE OF WOOD

If you still have wood, then you have a chance to recarve. What if you've carved away too much? Or turned an F into an E? It may mean starting again, and that's that.

But, bearing in mind that every part of a carving is relative to every other part, it is sometimes almost magically possible, by an adroit adjustment of parts or levels, to carve wood back on again…

Detail of a rococo confessional box in the Benedictine monastery church in Ettal, southern Germany. The repair here is clearly visible because of the colour difference. In repairing old carvings it is now standard practice not to hide the repair, but rather allow the viewer to differentiate old and new, while not causing a jarring note to the viewer's perception of the whole

CHAPTER 10

THE RETURNING

The image of this sculpture (Figs 10.1–10.4) came to me many years ago. I cannot remember now whether it came as a dream or vision, or whether the event needs nothing more than a 'good idea' to describe its origins. I do remember mulling it over while walking across a summer field and thinking I would need a *huge* log of something like elm in which to carve it, if I were to do it justice. Years later the idea was still returning to mind, and the elm log was always somewhere else.

I know it is a good habit to jot down ideas, catching them like slippery fishes as they swim briefly through our heads. Many I do, many I don't; and of the latter I am sure a fair proportion swim back into the depths, never a bubble to be seen again. Luckily, some images do return periodically, and this carving represents one such. I never recorded the idea as a sketch or model, but it has still returned again and again over the years, perhaps depending on the circumstances of my life, but not seeming to change very much.

Fig 10.1 *Right front view of The Returning on its pedestal*

Fig 10.2 *Left front view*

Fig 10.3 The three-quarter rear view shows how the cloak blends into the horse's mane

Fig 10.4 Back view of the carving

DESIGN

The image is of a warrior figure, perhaps a sort of king with no need to wear a crown. He erupts from the shadowy earth in front of me astride a great warhorse, wearing a plain helmet and wheeling a simple sword. His cape swirls from his shoulders back into the ground. The body of the warrior, his cape and the horse merge together, all somewhat undifferentiated. The lower half of the carving reflects this strong energy from which the torso seems to arise.

The body of the figure is immensely powerful, and yet the face is that of a fierce old man. Someone suggested it was 'Freudian', but then moved on to 'Jungian'. It is what it is, and I'm not sure I understand it. The important feeling for me is the sense of an ancient power returning again and again. So, all in all, calling it 'The Returning' seems as good a title as any.

Although I felt originally that carving it huge was the only way to do it justice, this thought always blocked me. I finally realized that if I waited any longer I would never catch this particular fish in any form that could be shared with other people. So when the image last returned I decided to attempt to capture it in a manageable size – manageable in terms of both the material to hand and the time that was available. I feel it was a bit like playing Mahler on a transistor radio, but at least it's now 'out there'.

I have not provided a working drawing, because I do not expect readers to copy this carving; it is more a question of witnessing my approach.

MODEL

Rather than draw the image on paper, I decided to sketch it three-dimensionally. The model, which I made in Plasticine, was more or less the intended size of the finished carving (see Fig 10.7).

I intended to use this model in several ways, along the lines described on page 46: for measuring wood, considering the strength and direction of the grain, calculating where waste wood should be removed at the outset, and generally helping to grasp the three-dimensional form. What I was *not* going to do – for the reasons mentioned on page 47 – was make a model in Plasticine and then copy it in wood.

I referred to the model in the early stages of carving; among other things, it helped me set the masses in the right places and establish the flow of lines in three dimensions as I wanted, preventing me from removing wood at an early stage that I might want later. After a while I found that I was looking less at the model, then hardly at all. For perhaps the last two thirds of the carving I didn't look at the model at all. It had done its job, and I was fully engaged with the carving process by this time.

WOOD

I chose a block of English oak for the subject. The figuring is delicate but present. Although not normally thought of as a suitable wood for detailed work, I find good-quality oak can take quite a lot of detail. Additionally, oak seemed an appropriately 'strong' wood, both in its colour and figuring and in its historical and cultural connotations. Elm, if available, would have been equally suitable.

There was a knot in the wood, and early on I had to decide whether to place it at the back (say, on the cape), or in a waste area so that I could cut it out – or to try and make a feature of it. I took the latter approach, and orientated the carving in the wood so that the knot was placed on the horse's forehead. This gave an earthiness to the horse's semi-abstract form (Fig 10.5).

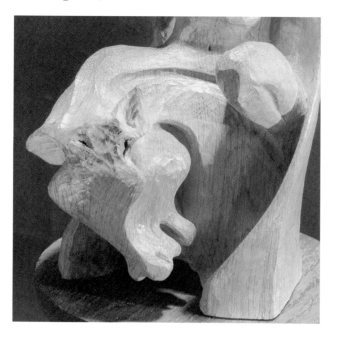

HOLDING

I knew there was to be some heavy preliminary mallet work, so for the main roughing out I sawed a square block into the base of the oak, and gripped this in a vice. When the work became lighter I cut this block off and moved the workpiece to a swivel-ball adjustable clamp. I protected my tools from the metal plate with a padding of plywood, fixing the workpiece to the clamp with two long, large screws (Fig 10.6).

Fig 10.6 Referring to the model to gauge the position of the screw holes, the wood is fixed to an adjustable holding device for most of the carving. The plywood prevents tools accidentally being damaged on the metal plate

CARVING

ROUGHING OUT

From my model I was able to calculate the removal of several large sections of wood with the bandsaw. I didn't want to commit myself to anything too exact at this stage and, since the size was small, I didn't need powered help to go further.

Fig 10.5 Rather than place the knot where it would be cut out, I took a gamble and placed it where I calculated the horse's forehead would be

Fig 10.7 *Ready to start: wood gripped by a waste block in the vice, model as a guide nearby*

Fig 10.8 *Preliminary roughing out with large gouge and mallet*

BOSTING IN

So all preparations are now made: the model is nearby for reference, the workpiece is clamped in the vice, strops and tools are to hand, and a cup of tea to steady the nerves; now the first cuts can be made (Fig 10.7).

Some vigorous carving with large gouges and mallet (Fig 10.8) establishes the relationship between the principal masses; the main planes and lines, and how they flow; and the general rhythm of the piece.

Refer to the model, and draw lines on the wood for guidance. In the photographs (Fig 10.8, for example) you can see these lines being drawn, cut away and redrawn. This is a very common and helpful carving practice.

After a while, you should find that the main masses of the carving are in the right places and the intended movement is becoming clear. At this point we can move on to a more refined bosting where these masses and planes are broken down further into their constituent parts. This means starting to carve the hollows deeper, and following the forms around into them (Fig 10.9).

A point mentioned elsewhere in this book, and worth emphasizing again here, is that it is almost always a mistake to create holes early on, unless you are very sure of their position and size. The holes tend to enlarge as you 'fiddle' with them. A better

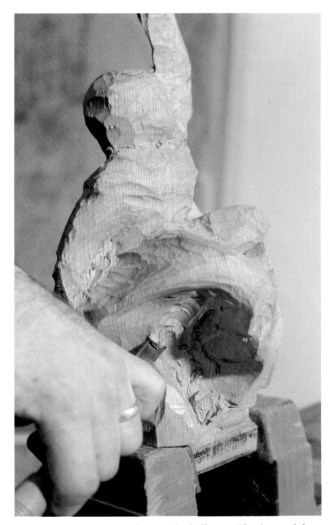

Fig 10.9 *Beginning to deepen the hollows. The form of the figure is now becoming visible*

Fig 10.10 *Always work the form and let the hollows take care of themselves, rather than deliberately making holes first and working the form to them. Here, the space beneath the right arm begins to open as the side of the body is shaped*

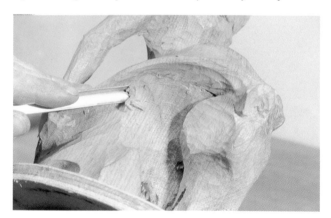

Fig 10.11 *Keeping things simple: details come at a later, more appropriate stage*

plan is to *carve the form around and into what will be the hole, and allow the hole to arise naturally.* In this way the hole seems to appear by itself (Fig 10.10).

Carving is a reductive process – it could be said to be analytical – moving through stages, each of which arises out of the previous one. Details follow naturally at the appropriate time as the supporting forms are established. So keep the carving flowing and simple at this stage (Fig 10.11).

MODELLING

It is another mistake (and one I point out to students again and again) to start putting in detail, which really belongs to the finished surface, too early. This will not only prematurely 'fix' the carving, but may possibly entail removing wood that will be needed later; and at best your work will most certainly have to be cut away, making it a waste of time and effort. So be aware of what is final detail and what is still part of the modelling (or even bosting-in) stage of a form.

On the whole, the modelling stage of this carving is mostly straightforward, needing the usual variety of tools. The cape is a little tricky; it is only about 2–3mm (¹⁄₁₆–¹⁄₈in) thick, and cut in quite deeply around the back of the body. After a while, the straight tool can no longer get into the hollow, especially in the lower part where the horse's head keeps getting in the way. Backbent gouges are useful here (Fig 10.12).

FLEXIBLE SHAFT

When I had shaped the horse's head I used a high-speed flexible drive shaft with a small spherical cutter to undercut the neck (Fig 10.13). None of my conventional carving tools would do this job. I also used the cutter to hollow inside the horse's mouth. In both cases I was trying to get that bit more shadow. (Please note the advice on using a flexible-shaft machine on page 77.)

Fig 10.12 *A backbent tool cleans the inside of the cape*

Fig 10.13 The horse's stylized jaw crease is undercut with a rotary cutter to get more shadow; none of my other tools had the right profile for this particular operation

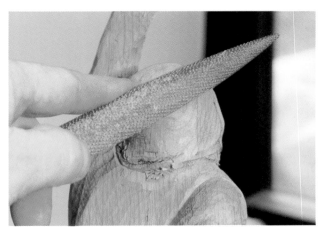

Fig 10.14 To get a sense of form in the helmet, a rasp can be used first

Fig 10.15 The rasped surface is afterwards refined and finished with carving tools

RIFFLERS

Sometimes I like to work a surface with a rasp or riffler before finishing it off with carving tools; this method seems to give a better feel for the underlying form. For example, the riffler is able to sweep smoothly around the dome of the helmet, so giving the required form, in a way that would be difficult to achieve with a gouge (Fig 10.14). The surface can then be cleaned over with carving tools (Fig 10.15).

HAND AND SWORD

Bearing in mind what I said about carving the form first and letting the spaces take care of themselves, bring the sword hand close to its final shape, forming the recess where the sword should sit (Fig 10.16), before boring the hole (Fig 10.17).

Fig 10.16 Shaping the sword hand: waste is cut away with a coping saw

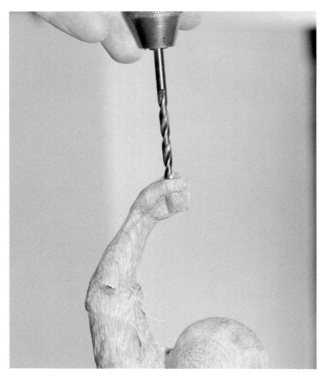

Fig 10.17 The hole for the sword is bored after the shape of the hand has been defined. Work on the hand while the rest of the arm still has the supporting strength of waste wood

The sword itself is made at the very end, using a sliver of oak from the original block of wood. The sword is in two parts, with a separate pommel fitted beneath, and the main part of the sword ending in a tightly fitting spigot to sit in the hand.

DETAILING

As the carving progresses, shapes can be refined more and more, and details can be put in: some hair in the mane that is gripped by the returning warrior's right hand (Fig 10.18); anatomical features such as muscles and bones; the helmet and face. These details almost arise out of the preceding stages. Smaller tools will be required, many of them fishtails, especially for work around the face (Fig 10.19). Larger surfaces can be coaxed to a finish with flatter gouges.

The whole carving is worked to a finish with the tools, without the use of sandpaper. If nothing else, the tool cuts add vigour (Fig 10.20). You can only achieve a good tooled finish if you keep your edges razor-sharp. I try to keep all the cuts clean as I go along, so there is no need to tidy up at the end.

Fig 10.18 Final details include a fringe of the horse's mane, gripped by the warrior's hand

Fig 10.19 A detail of the face, strong and old

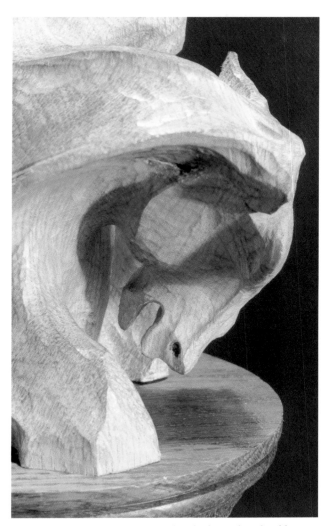

Fig 10.20 *Detail of the horse's head; the toolwork adds a certain vigour to the surface*

When all the toolwork is completed, I make a point of taking the carving outside the workshop and checking over the surface with an entirely different lighting. This shows up any tears or blemishes which might need cleaning up.

FINISHING

I tapped oak plugs into the screw holes beneath and trimmed them off; I know they are unlikely to be seen, but it's always best to do a tidy job. Some people always look…

Lastly I brushed the wood with several coats of thin beeswax, to which a little carnauba wax had been added, and buffed it up.

STAND

There are several reasons for mounting a carving: for example, to display the carving better, to help support a fragile piece of work, or to make a further artistic statement. Not all carvings need a display stand, but I decided this one did – not least to lift it physically higher. After some preliminary sketches I settled on a short classical column, alluding to the distant past age from which the figure has arisen.

The column stand is turned from reclaimed oak, with all the woodworm holes and marks left in. After the turning and fluting I 'distressed' the wood even further to make it look fittingly ancient. A lighter brown stain was applied to the top of the column and a darker one at the bottom. The whole was then given a few coats of teak oil and waxed.

CONCLUSION

To me it is a curious privilege to be able to capture an image that has arisen from my unconscious.

There is no doubt that the returning figure has changed considerably from the original presence in my mind: solidifying from something darker and more nebulous into a solid form; being constrained by the nature of wood, the carving process and my own carving ability. I am sure that if I carved the idea again, it would appear different.

I think woodcarving bestows so many opportunities, possibilities and even privileges on the carver. The final carving may be smaller than I had in mind, but at least the perpetually returning figure can stay a while.

SOURCES OF INSPIRATION

NETS AND MAGPIES

Thinking of what to carve next can be a major frustration for some carvers. Many students copy the work of others (drawings, photographs, paintings, carvings) from the beginning, and find the transition to designs entirely of their own either intimidating or disheartening. The answer in both cases is to feel inspired.

In chapter 7 of *Relief Carving in Wood: A Practical Introduction*, I discuss where ideas come from and recommend keeping:

1 **A scrapbook**: fill this with anything which grabs your attention – cuttings from magazines, say, and pictures of other carvings, etc.

2 **A notebook**: fill this with ideas, thoughts, critiques of carvings, etc.

3 **A sketchbook**: fill this with drawings and sketches related to the other two books, and anything you see.

Whether you want simply to produce attractive objects, to carve furniture, or to engage in the personal development of the artist, together these books will form a great pool of ideas through which to drag your net.

In particular, study closely the work of other carvers past and present, in churches, galleries, books. Look closely at what they have done. Study the use of the three elements in all woodcarvings: the design, the way it is played out in the material, they way it has been executed. Could you do better? Would you do it differently? Would you have done

the opposite? Study critically. *Ideas* are free jewels for you to take, magpie-like, to your nest, even if the manner and work belong to the original artist.

Look at stonecarvers too: wood and stone carving are similar in that they are both glyptic, reductive processes. Look at sculpture in general, for design, for purpose.

The works of living woodcarvers can be found in books and magazines – study them critically.

Casting our net more widely: recent carvers such as Eric Gill and Henry Moore are well known, as are Michelangelo, Riemenschneider and Gibbons, but what about Ernst Barlach (German, 1870–1938), Gustav Vigeland (Norwegian, 1869–1943), Ivan Meštrović (Croatian, 1883–1962), for example?

Greek and Egyptian carvings are familiar, and we tend to see European art and culture as the standard by which to judge all others, but what about the fine sculptural work from Africa, Mexico and Central America? And while Europeans were chopping wood for fires in the Dark Ages, a truly unsurpassed tradition of carving it flourished in Japan. The great age of Japanese wood sculpture lasted from about 600 to 1300 CE, and culminated in a family of geniuses: Kaiki (late twelfth century), his son Unkei (1151–1223), and *his* sons, including Tankei (1173–1256).

Thanks to photography you can browse through time and space to view a vast range of carved work. Don't be overawed by these illustrious names and works, or feel you are in competition with them; just breathe them in and have joy.

Inspiration is not so much an external force as the ability of the mind and heart to make use of what they see and feel. Detail of a pietà in polychromed oak, about 1400, Bayerisches Nationalmuseum, Munich

CHAPTER 11

OLD WOMAN'S HEAD

This simple carving (Figs 11.1–11.3) started life as a small doodle in clay, and not as a ready-carved image in my head, as did the sculpture in the last chapter. Even more than The Returning, the idea involved a 'translation' of its modelled forms into wood. Some thoughts about this are discussed in Modelling on pages 46–7.

Sometimes, instead of on paper, I sketch ideas in clay. Carvers tend to find this especially useful if they are interested in forms and interpretations of them, rather than simple representation. If ever you are lost for an idea, try playing with a lump of clay or Plasticine and see what turns up.

Even though this carving is in high relief, I think it demonstrates many of the fundamental principles of carving in the round.

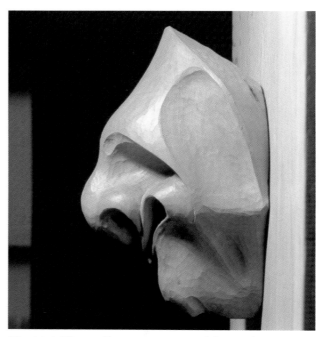

Fig 11.2 *The profile is very strong and distorted*

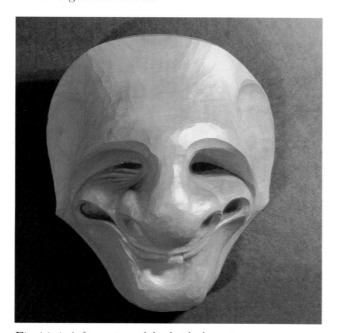

Fig 11.1 *A front view of the finished carving*

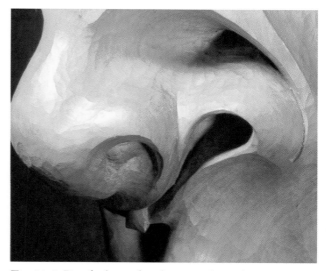

Fig 11.3 *Detail of nostril and corner of mouth*

DESIGN

THE IDEA

It was while I was making a larger model in clay that I found I had 'doodled' this small clay head (Fig 11.4), taking hardly any time and without thinking much what I was doing. Even now I am not even sure who it was meant to be. Was it a crone with one tooth or actually a fat medieval baker? Or something like the cartoon-strip layabout Andy Capp, with a dangling cigarette end rather than a tooth?

I liked particularly the roundness of the forms, the echo in shape between nostrils and mouth, and the way these in turn were reflected in an opposite direction by the eyes. The eyes themselves were merely deep crevices merging into folds in the cheeks. I was engaged by its garrulous humour and wondered whether, by turning the small model into a larger carving, I could keep the features I liked. So I had a go – still without thinking much about it.

WOOD

The wood I used was air-dried pear – almost half a log. In this carving the abstracted forms are most important. Pearwood is quite a bland wood, with negligible figuring; however, it has a warm, Cheddar-cheese-like appearance and carves well.

After cleaning off the bark and removing the sapwood edges, I flattened the back. This was partly to allow for fixing to the holding device, and partly because it would be quite difficult to finish off the back once the carving had been completed. Almost without exception, I make it the rule with all carvings to finish the back or base first, as part of the preparation before carving proper.

HOLDING

The deckchair stand described on pages 20–1 was perfect for this small carving, which was fixed through the back with a carver's screw (Fig 11.5), although I also used the main tilting bench at times. The carving is actually quite deep and three-dimensional, and having the face upright in front of

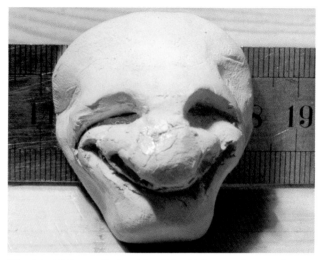

Fig 11.4 The small clay 'doodle' which turned out to be my working model

Fig 11.5 The bandsawn block fixed to the deckchair stand with a carver's screw, ready to start

me kept out distortion from perspective and allowed a certain sense of intimacy.

The back of the forehead and cap was 'backed off' (cut away behind) towards the end, as can be seen in Fig 11.2, and this involved a change in the method of holding, which will be described later.

CARVING

ROUGHING OUT

Some major cuts can be made with the bandsaw, estimating from the model. The workpiece is then fixed to the work surface, ready for carving.

In order to reproduce, or at least come close to reproducing, the original you want to copy, you need to position the model so its perspective is the same as that of the carving block in front of you. I wasn't interested in an exact enlargement or copy, so at no stage did I take measurements. Placing the model nearby, so you can look from one to the other and make comparisons without moving more than your eyes, allows you to trust your judgement.

If a close copy were needed, then establishing reference points by cross-measuring would be the only safe way of proceeding.

BOSTING IN

The first stage in this and every carving is to take the largest tools possible and remove the largest and simplest lumps of wood from the block (Fig 11.6). In this early stage, concentrate on the overall shape and the major changes in plane; try to remove the squareness of the sides by cutting away the corners, and 'push away' the wood to deepen recesses (Fig 11.7). Note in Fig 11.2 how far back the corners of the mouth are from the tip of the nose: a lot of wood needs to come away here as the sides of the nose emerge. The forehead slopes back both above and to the sides, taking back the outer corners of the eyes; so here, too, much wood must be taken away very early in the carving.

Bosting in, as I repeat many times in this book, is always the most important stage in a carving (see Notes on the Carving Process on page 24): on this everything else depends. And although the surface will be gone over again later, it is worth cutting as cleanly as possible, as the photographs show, in this early stage (see Clean Cutting on page 68). It saves time in the long run, and gives a clearer idea of the underlying form.

As you get further into the carving you can start placing masses more accurately: the wings of the nose, and lumps where the ends of the mouth will be, for example.

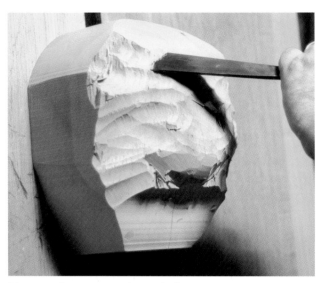

Fig 11.6 *Large gouges begin the bosting in*

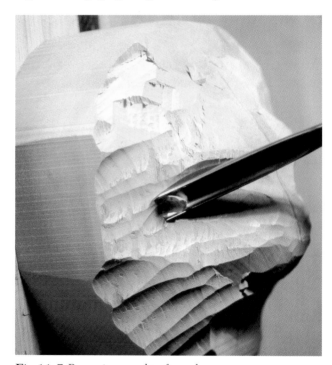

Fig 11.7 *Removing wood to form the eye recesses*

Another important general principle in carving is to *proceed from the form into the space*. Don't just go digging holes – they get out of control, and commonly will end up too large. So, for the eye sockets, shape the lumps for the ends of the mouth and just continue over and into the eye, visualizing the surface beneath the gouge. In this way the form will be left rounded; this carving has a lot of full, convex masses.

Once you have the main shape of the head and are happy with the placement of the ends of the mouth, use a V-tool to lay the line of the mouth itself (Fig 11.8). You can now turn to the ends of the mouth and the chin (Fig 11.9). As you can see from the photographs, the surface is still cleanly cut.

MODELLING

All this time I was referring to the little model to guide the carving. After a while – probably about a third of the way in – I found I was happy with the carving and had stopped looking.

The lower lip is left full around the front of the carving, leaving enough wood standing proud to form the tooth as the lip is taken back around it. The best tools for carving the tooth, lips and lip crevice were the V-tool and skew chisel (Fig 11.10).

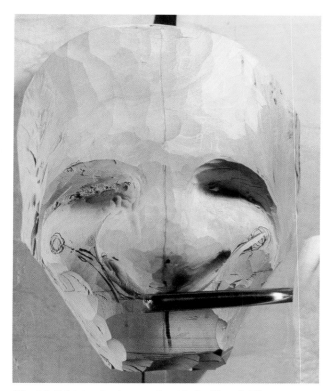

Fig 11.8 Lining in the mouth with the V-tool. The top part of the face and the nose are already in place

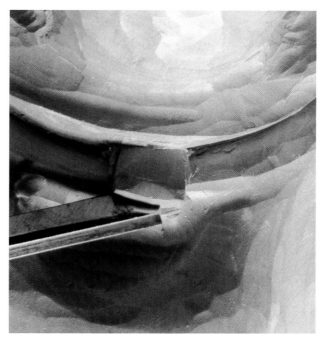

Fig 11.10 Carving the tooth with a V-tool

Fig 11.11 shows the carved face 'caught'. This is a stage I like, as it usually means that the hardest struggle is over and I am now heading into the home straight with a fair chance of winning. You will notice pencil lines in this and other photographs: I continually draw, carve away and redraw guidelines (even notes to myself) as I go along – again a very useful practice.

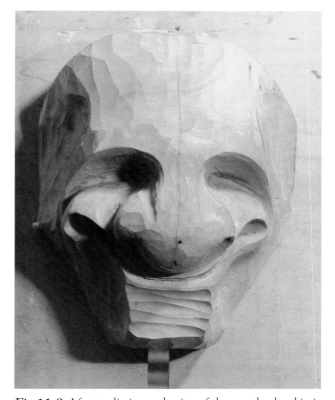

Fig 11.9 After preliminary shaping of the mouth, the chin is pushed back to arrive at the correct profile

The main job now is to deepen all the recesses: the eyes (Fig 11.12), nostrils and mouth (Fig 11.13).

The eyes can be readily accessed from the side, and need only a small deep gouge to clean up the back crease. There is a plane from the sides of the mouth right into the back of the eye which needs to be kept full.

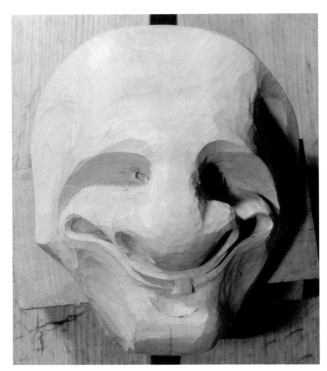

Fig 11.11 *The face has now been 'caught'. Final modelling and detailing can begin from this stage*

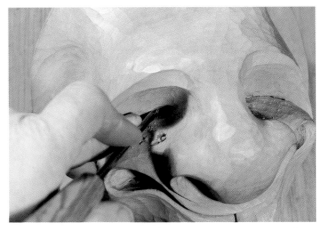

Fig 11.12 *The eyes are very deeply set in their creases, but are easy to get to from the side*

Fig 11.13 *At the corners of the mouth, small bent gouges are needed to clean up the bottoms of the recesses*

The nose and mouth need tight, small frontbent gouges to get in cleanly and deeply. When using these tools, be careful not to lever them too heavily against the edge of the hole, or the wood grain may break here. This was a particular problem when the collar of the Shirt (Chapter 8) was carved.

Now go back to check over the work and smooth the final surface with the flattest possible gouges. I felt the soft tooling mimicked the soft, crumpled appearance of the original clay model.

In order to get at the back of the carving and undercut around the forehead or cap, I had to take the workpiece off the tilting bench and 'hang' it backside uppermost off the bench by the longest carving screw I had (Fig 11.14). Before this, however, I was able to remove a satisfyingly large slice of waste using the bandsaw with its table tilted.

FINISHING

I brushed in several thin coats of beeswax and buffed them to give the pearwood a lovely warm colour. A toothbrush was particularly handy for the crevices.

CONCLUSION

Although I like this rather bizarre little carving, now it is finished I think it lacks the sort of slob-like bulk that the clay model – even though small – expressed. The original had more of the sketch about it, and was more asymmetrical and more 'crusty', especially around the nose; and this surface texture adds a lot to the personality of the doodle.

In this carving the idea, or design, led the other elements which, in a way, had to rise to meet it. The difference between a carving and a model in clay is quite marked: the stronger changes of plane that characterize the carving are a major difference, and to me it seems that what was a simple, unconscious act has become more rational and clear-cut.

But it was fun to do. How about doodling something yourself and carving it?

Fig 11.14 This is where the carver's screw really comes into its own: to get at the back of the carving, I hung it from the bench with the aid of a strong clamp and blocks of scrap wood

STUDENTS' PROBLEMS

HARD TRUTHS: GUITARS AND CHOICES

In the learning process, students – even experienced ones – do seem to turn up with the same problems again and again, as if they get stuck in a holding pattern and can't move on. I mention many such problems throughout this and my other books, and Gino Masero (see Chapter 13) had his own short list. I would like to focus on my two all-time favourites: it is a difficult situation for students when they both occur simultaneously.

SHARPENING

You will not get far at playing the guitar until you can tune it – and sharpening is just as crucial to carving. Luckily, sharpening is not difficult to master – it really isn't. I show students and they usually pick it up quickly. The aims are straightforward, the means to the end graduated and logical. With some care and attention, keen edges are easy to have, and maintain. So what's the problem? It's this:

Students who only carve occasionally will find the sharp edges of good tools last a long time; they might not even notice the slow creep of dullness or a rounded bevel, and when they do they might not be bothered to deal with it, just then. Eventually, when they *do* feel a strange, guilty urge to resharpen, a long time has passed since they last gave sharpening any thought. They have understandably forgotten what they did; they always seem to be going back to square one.

If you recognize this, the only real answer is to carve more – and to understand the importance of bothering. If you cannot spend more time carving

and are experiencing this problem with keeping tools sharp, compile your own notebook on 'how to sharpen', and lay out the method that works well for you. *Keep a diary of what you did the last time you found you had forgotten* – you will need it again.

PRACTICE

Many students expect rewards without investment. Practice means repeating a skill over and over again until it becomes habitual, building up more and more, and so developing as a carver. This needs time. Without time for practice, competence in tool handling, or the ability to visualize, will remain low, and so will confidence. Carvings take a long time to finish, and the work can be tedious and frustrating.

But that's the way it is: there is no magic pill. Those who practice make more progress, and are often thought to have an extra 'gift' or talent. They might have – but who can tell, unless we practice the same amount? Experienced carvers who make it 'look easy' are, more than anything else, drawing on their reserves of practice.

Everyone has the same amount of time. However, individual time is proportioned out according to our priorities, whether by choice or by obligation. If you really *cannot* do more, then you cannot, and that's that. The point is that such conditions directly affect your ability to carve, what you can manage, and even your attitude to sharpening. But you have to accept this and cut your cloth to suit. Take on smaller, simpler projects that can be completed quickly, rather than long ones that can frustrate through slow progress. Draw and model when you cannot carve (see Drawing on page 34 and Modelling on pages 46–7), and soak up carvings (see Sources of Inspiration on page 114). Try and make your workplace easy to be in and comfortable; perhaps it's possible to carve on a small scale in a corner inside the house, rather than curse and avoid the cold garage bench.

A rather sinister-looking wren. Interesting design and good use of wood grain, but the student should really try it again to get the beak and eye more wren-like, and perhaps add more wood below the bird to counter the impression of tipping forward. Unfortunately, most students will put all their eggs in one basket, and rarely repeat a carving until they get it right

CHAPTER 12

BUTTERFLIES

These butterflies (Figs 12.1 and 12.2) are fairly easy to carve but do need a light touch.

In this project we are not trying to make an exact replica of a butterfly – and why should anyone? It is more a rejoicing in butterflies through the medium of wood. A real butterfly is an amazingly delicate thing (Fig 12.3), often with incredible colours and patterns, and with flat wings. If we were to reproduce the butterfly exactly in wood, with the true flatness of its wings and without the brilliant displays of colour, we would not only be emphasizing this flatness but also producing something quite boring. We therefore have to modify the real form a bit to compensate for the medium we are using. This makes the task one of suggestion: to shape the wings in a way which is not trying to copy their exact, true form, but to suggest to the viewer lightness, delicacy, a hint of movement and the suspicion that perhaps it could fly. Just for a moment we hope the viewer will forget it is wood, or perhaps confuse wood and butterfly in their mind.

DESIGN

RESEARCH

As with all carvings, it is essential to have a clear idea of what you want to carve, before you lay into the piece of wood. You might think you know what a butterfly looks like, until you come to draw one, let alone carve one; so first study the subject a little. There is no need to imitate Mrs Beeton by catching

Fig 12.2 *The same moth displayed on carved and bent beechwood leaves in a glass dome*

Fig 12.1 *A moth carved in lacewood*

Fig 12.3 *A real peacock butterfly: the subject for the carving*

one – there are plenty of illustrations and photographs in wildlife or nature books from which you can select a model. When the opportunity arises, observe the real thing and perhaps make a few sketches.

DISPLAYING

Before starting on this project, consider the advice at the end of this chapter on ways of mounting the butterfly. This needs to be considered as part of the whole work.

In my carving, the butterfly is posed so that the parts that are viewed are the back, the head and the wings. The legs, extraordinarily thin in reality, are hidden from view and do not need to be carved. They can be implied, though, by setting the butterfly a little away from whatever it is mounted on. This gives a sense of space (and therefore legs) underneath. The degree to which you elaborate the carving, having relieved it from its background, is up to you. I will show you how you can thin the wings to a degree of translucency and separate the front wings from the back, but you can stop before this and still create a very good effect.

THE SUBJECT

The model we will follow here is that of a peacock butterfly, which is quite a simple shape (see Fig 12.3); but of course there are many butterflies that will do. A lot of moths work well, such as the hawk moth, but remember that there are some distinctive differences between moths and butterflies, for example in the shape of the antennae (see Figs 12.4*b* and 12.6).

DRAWING

Make a life-size outline from the photo or drawing. Try for symmetry, but don't be a slave to it. Fig 12.4*a* is a full-sized working drawing for the carving illustrated here. The tiny irregularities of the wing edges have been stylized into appropriate but bold curves to fit the available carving tools; this works better than fiddly details. A standard carving practice is to match the design to the tools when matching the tools to the design is not possible.

The butterfly is drawn on to the wood after the angle of the wings has been sawn or carved in, and before starting the carving proper.

25mm (1in)   10mm (⅜in)

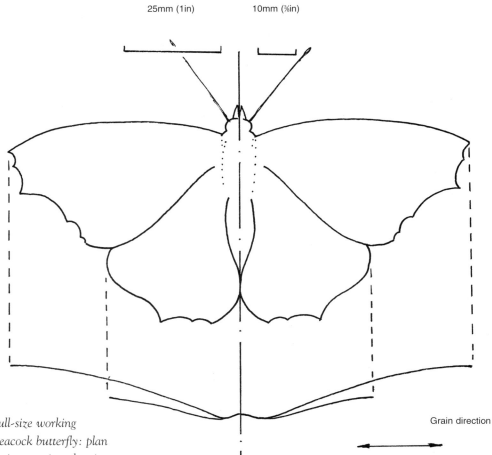

Fig 12.4 (a) Full-size working drawing of the peacock butterfly: plan view and schematic rear view showing the angle at which the wings are set

Grain direction

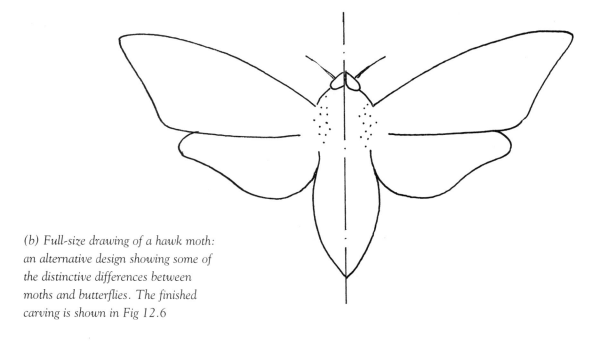

(b) Full-size drawing of a hawk moth: an alternative design showing some of the distinctive differences between moths and butterflies. The finished carving is shown in Fig 12.6

WOOD

These carved butterflies are a good way to use offcuts. You will need a piece measuring about 140mm along the grain by 80mm across and 50mm deep (5½ x 3¼ x 2in). This depth allows for holding the work in the first stage of the carving.

I am using an offcut of tight-grained lime for the demonstration because, with an oil finish, a simple but very effective translucency is possible. This gives a particularly pleasing sense of thinness and lightness. For the best colour, choose a piece with close grain from near the heart of the tree.

You could, of course, exploit knots, spalting, and the prominent grain of many other woods, such as lacewood. Be careful not to overdo it, though: some woods, especially dense exotic ones, can appear very heavy and thick, even when carved thinly. This is a common fault with marquetry-style or assembled butterflies: they can appear thick and heavy. Also, strong, violent grain can be confusing in a simple shape. This may sound paradoxical, given that butterflies can be so exotically coloured, but remember my introductory comments: *this is not a butterfly but a woodcarving*. Don't go over the top – but do experiment.

JOINING

If you are using a figured wood such as lacewood, you may like to consider splitting a piece with nice grain so that the two pieces can be joined at an angle with a tight, rubbed, butt joint (known as a **bookmatched** joint: Figs 12.5 and 12.6). In this way you can mirror the pattern between the wings as in the real thing.

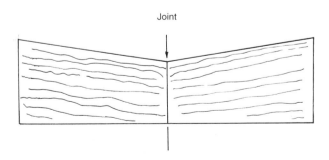

Fig 12.5 *Joining two slices of wood to produce a pair of wings with matched grain*

Fig 12.6 *Hawk moth in lacewood, carved from two pieces joined along the centre line to match the grain*

Joining wood is also a way of setting the wing angles, which is the first practical job to be done.

HOLDING

The way the work is held is best described as we proceed; it progresses from simply holding the initial block in a vice, to holding a small part of it, to working with the carving held in our hands.

CARVING

TOOLS

This is a list of (straight) carving tools used in this particular project, which should match my working drawing exactly:

1 No. 3 x 3, 5, 6, 10, 19mm (⅛, 3⁄16, ¼, ⅜, ¾in)

2 No. 4 x 10mm (⅜in)

3 No. 5 x 10, 16mm (⅜, ⅝in)

4 No. 6 x 6mm (¼in)

5 No. 7 x 8mm (5⁄16in)

6 No. 8 x 5, 8mm (3⁄16, 5⁄16in)

7 No. 39 x 6mm (¼in) V-tool.

You will also need:

• a coping saw for cutting away the background;

- a Stanley or similar knife with which to prepare the antennae and mouthparts;

- a small awl, which can be made from a needle mounted in a handle or from a ground-down masonry nail (Fig 12.7);

- a small vice to hold the work. Carvers' chops work well if available, but even one of those small vices that clamp to the bench will work well enough, since the work is quite light.

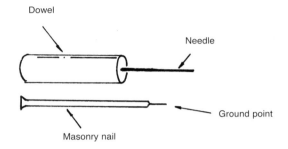

Fig 12.7 Two kinds of home-made awl for boring holes to take antennae, mouthparts and mounting spigot

Wing angles

You need to decide the angle of the wings. The cross section included in Fig 12.4 shows the wings spread at a slight angle from the horizontal. If you make them too upright you will have to work out some satisfactory way of making the legs; too flat, and the form loses some sense of movement.

Grip the wood block firmly in the vice, allowing at least 25mm (1in) to project unobstructed above the vice (Fig 12.8).

Fig 12.8 The wood held in the vice for roughing out; an offcut is sufficient for this project

With your largest flat gouge, cut down from either side towards the midline (Fig 12.9). Then slice away the waste across the grain (Fig 12.10) until you are left with the correct wing angle (Fig 12.11). Don't make a V-shape where the two sides meet; flow smoothly from one wing to the other. The area where they meet will eventually be formed into the body of the butterfly. All this work could be done with a narrow-bladed bandsaw.

Fig 12.9 Creating the angle of the wings by cutting with the grain from where their tips will be

Fig 12.10 Clearing out the middle, across the grain; make the junction between the wings a smooth curve

Fig 12.11 The surface of the wood ready for marking out the butterfly shape

MARKING OUT

Transfer the drawing via tracing paper to the wood, either by using carbon paper or by scribbling over the back of the tracing in soft pencil (Figs 12.12 and 12.13). You may find it helpful to draw a centre line. Bear in mind that the pencil marks are only guidelines for your eye to feel into.

Fig 12.12 Transferring the drawing on to the wood with carbon paper

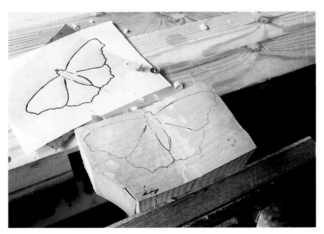

Fig 12.13 The wood held in the vice, marked out and ready to begin carving

STAGE 1: LOW RELIEF CARVING

It is best to consider the subject as a low relief carving, with stylized details, subsequently undercut (pierced) so much that the butterfly 'takes off' from the background. (Grinling Gibbons is said to have used a similar technique with his famous lace cravat carvings; it is a way of making the work look much more complicated for relatively little extra effort.)

GROUNDING OUT

Quickly clear away the background to leave the butterfly standing proud:

1 Take the V-tool and run a trench around the whole butterfly about 3mm (⅛in) outside the edge of the drawing (Fig 12.14).

2 Clear away the background with a large flat gouge (Fig 12.15). You can leave quite a rough background – don't bother to finish it level, as we are eventually going to cut it away.

3 Repeat these two steps until the background is recessed at least 13mm (½in) below the top surface of the wings (Fig 12.16).

Fig 12.14 The preliminary V-tool trench around the outline

Fig 12.15 Clearing away the background with the large flat gouge

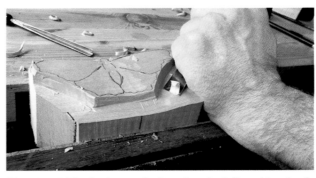

Fig 12.16 The background relieved to the full working depth

SETTING IN

Use the appropriate gouges to outline or 'set in' the butterfly neatly up to the drawn lines (Fig 12.17). Whichever shape of butterfly you are carving, try to match the curves of the tools to the lines you have drawn, on both sides equally: this gives the work a crisp, symmetrical look. Set the edge in vertically and don't undercut yet.

The next job is to carve the upper surface of the butterfly itself.

MODELLING

1 Start by defining the various parts: the two wings on either side, the abdomen, and a lump for the head (Fig 12.18).

2 From here turn to shaping the upper surface (Fig 12.19). You will find you need mainly the very flat tools – there is little wood to remove. Don't make the wings too undulating, but put in a delicate curve so that the wings tilt up a little at the edge. Real wings are dead flat, as I said above; but for the purposes of carving we are trying to give a sense of aliveness, as if the butterfly were getting ready to move. Give the thorax a slightly rougher texture than the wings; in real life it is quite hairy.

3 Work towards the head (Fig 12.20) and carve the two bulbous eyes. Leave a flat 'nose' where the mouthparts will be put in later.

4 As the two pairs of wings are formed, allow the front ones to overlap the rear ones a little, and actually start to undercut with the V-tool so as to create a shadow (Fig 12.21). If you don't want to separate the wings, this is as far as you need go just here. If you do wish to separate them, continue to undercut until you have an overlap of about 3mm ($\frac{1}{8}$in). You need to undercut far enough in under the top wing so that when the back of the butterfly is carved away the undercut becomes a hole separating the wings. You don't need to get the bottom of the cut clean in this case, as it will be removed in due course.

5 The groove separating the abdomen from the rear wings should not be too deep – unless you intend to free the wings from the body, which does not seem necessary in this case (Fig 12.22).

Fig 12.17 *Setting in the wings with gouges of appropriate shape*

Fig 12.18 *Starting to shape the surface: separating the wings with a V-tool*

Fig 12.19 *Modelling the wings*

Fig 12.20 *Beginning to shape the head and eyes*

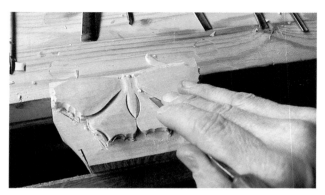

Fig 12.21 *Undercutting the top wing with a tilted V-tool*

Fig 12.22 *Cutting the groove which separates the lower wing from the abdomen*

Fig 12.23 *Now the top surface is finished, undercutting the wings away from the background can begin – this helps in the subsequent cutting out*

Fig 12.24 *Using a coping saw to cut the butterfly free from the background*

Finish the whole surface of the wings cleanly with the gouges, taking very fine shavings so as to merge one facet into the next. Try to make the finishing strokes meaningful. If your tools are really sharp the surface should not need sanding, and indeed a slightly irregular surface catches the light and gives the form a little more life.

Sanding perfectly smooth tends to leave a hard, eggshell-like surface. However, if your preference is to sand, then try to remove any scratch marks by dampening and finishing finely, as scratches will show when the oil finish is applied.

UNDERCUTTING

Undercut the background around the butterfly quite deeply (Fig 12.23); this is a preliminary to cutting away the background in the following stage.

What you should have now is a finished low relief carving of the butterfly with a rough background. Apart from the background, do make sure everything is nicely finished so you don't have to touch it further.

STAGE 2: REMOVING THE BACKGROUND

With the work held in the vice, use the coping saw to cut out the butterfly, cutting parallel to the faces of the wings and as close to them as you dare (Fig 12.24). Leave a square lump projecting underneath in the middle, about 13mm (½in) across (Fig 12.25). The butterfly will be held by this little block in subsequent stages; it is eventually either pared off or modified for mounting.

Fig 12.25 *A projecting piece is left to hold the carving while the underside is worked*

The final stage of sawing is tricky, as the work is now quite fragile. Using some small pieces of softwood as packing, clamp the relatively strong body in the vice and go carefully.

STAGE 3: THE UNDERSIDE

You should now be holding something like a butterfly in your hand, finished on the top surface and roughly, but neatly, sawn underneath. The next task is to carve away and clean up the under surface of the wings.

Hold the butterfly by the projecting piece on the underside (Fig 12.26). Make sure your tools are very sharp, because the amount of pressure you can safely use gets less and less as you proceed!

Start paring away at the outer edges of the wings and move towards the body; this retains the strength as long as possible. Begin with the small no. 5 gouge and finish with the no. 3s, following the contours of the upper surface. Take your time: work evenly and systematically, using a slicing stroke. With sharp tools you can work across the grain (Fig 12.27).

HOW THIN IS IT?

Well it's definitely too thin when you come out the other side, if that's any help! Use your fingers to gauge the thickness, and keep eyeing across the edge. Position a spotlight to shine on the back of the wood (Fig 12.28). You will see the wood become translucent as it gets thinner, and you can use the level of translucency as a guide to the thickness.

Be particularly careful as you separate the wings, and around the groove that separates wings from body. The upper wing should overlap the lower – there should be no visible gap when you look straight on at the upper surface of the wings.

A little raw linseed oil rubbed on the wings enhances the translucence and allows you to carve even thinner. Keep the oil away from the head and the projecting lump beneath, where glue will be used. You can go to paper thickness with good wood.

As the wings get thinner they will start to flex and bend; and the amount of wood left to hold the butterfly gets less and less! It can get quite exciting, not to say nerve-racking. Go with the flexing of the wood, and keep your cutting edges keen.

Fig 12.26 *Holding the butterfly in carver's chops by means of the projecting piece*

Fig 12.27 *Finishing the undersides of the wings*

Fig 12.28 *Using a spotlight to show the thickness (by translucence) as the lower wing is carved*

HAND-HOLDING

At some point you will have to do away with the vice altogether and hold the butterfly in your hand, supporting and manipulating the cut of the carving tool with the thumb (Figs 12.29 and 12.30). Remember *always to work away from the hand*; then there is no danger of cutting yourself. Fig 12.31 shows the final stages.

Fig 12.29 *Use your hands to hold the butterfly in the final stages, supporting delicate cuts with the thumb*

Fig 12.30 *Wings getting thinner; the projecting vice-hold has yet to be removed*

Fig 12.31 *The holding block has now been removed; always work* away *from your hands and fingers*

Finish off the underside of the abdomen, giving it a slight downward flex. Keep everything clean, and pare away the central lump to form a small protuberance into which the mounting spigot will be inserted. At this stage you can stop holding your breath! Make sure the edges of the wings are crisp and clean; a little rolled-up sandpaper, very fine, may help here.

STAGE 4: ANTENNAE, MOUTHPARTS AND MOUNTING SPIGOT

Here we have a change of material: There is nothing like bamboo for grain strength in thinness.

I made the feelers or antennae from slivers of bamboo cane, thinned as far as possible with the Stanley knife (Figs 12.32 and 12.33). Again, always work away from your hands. Remember that moths have different antennae from butterflies.

Fig 12.32 *Paring the bamboo parts to shape with a Stanley knife*

Fig 12.33 *Mouthparts, antennae and mounting spigot ready for assembly*

The mouth piece was whittled from a larger piece of bamboo, leaving a small spigot for inserting into the butterfly.

A final little dowel is needed which goes into the body underneath, supporting the butterfly so that it seems to hover away from the surface on which it will be mounted (Fig 12.34).

Make the holes at the appropriate angles with the small awl and glue the various pieces in (Fig 12.35). The round tips on the ends of the feelers can be imitated by dipping the very ends into PVA wood glue and allowing it to dry as tiny blobs. (Luckily the butterfly is not flying very far.)

FINISHING

The butterfly is now complete, and when the glue is dry the wood can be saturated with raw linseed oil thinned with a little turpentine. Either brush it on, or dip the carving for a while into a small tub of oil. Wipe off the excess and apply a coat of thin beeswax when dry.

DISPLAY

There are rich possibilities for mounting to exploit the surprise value of this carving. However, these butterflies are obviously fragile and people will use the 'how-far-will-it-bend' test for thinness – especially on the antennae – so displaying in a dome is a good idea. It keeps the dust off, too.

Glass domes can be bought from specialist suppliers of craft equipment. A word of warning here: choose the dome first, or at least know the dimensions, and plan the size of the carving and mounting to fit, not the other way round!

A piece of hedge wood looks good, with the little dowel underneath the butterfly fitted into a matching hole. The hedge wood can also be shellacked or oiled, waxed and fixed to a wooden base (Fig 12.36).

CONCLUSION

The choice of material is crucial to this carving, as is designing with the grain in mind. And then again, a good technique and sharp tools are needed. So all in all this is a good example of the three elements coming together neatly in a carving – and a fine challenge!

Fig 12.34 *Side view of the finished butterfly, showing how it is mounted so as to hover above the surface*

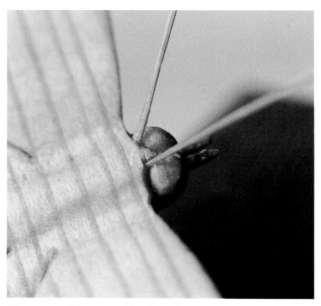

Fig 12.35 *Close-up of head, with antennae and mouthparts glued in place*

Fig 12.36 *The finished butterfly, with its friend, mounted in a glass dome*

CHAPTER 13

GINO MASERO

1915–1995

Gino Masero in 1994

Gino Masero demonstrating at the First Church and Schools Exhibition, Olympia, 1964. His tilting bench, on which mine is based, is visible at left

When I am asked to give a 'pen portrait' of myself for use in my woodcarving books or magazine articles, I always say that I 'owe my formative start to the master carver Gino Masero'. Since this fortunate beginning, I have learned – and hope I can always learn – from a wide range of people over the years, and have studied closely every carving and every piece of writing on carving that has come my way. So I do see myself as self-taught – as all carvers are – but the fact is that he started me off, and I have only ever added to what Gino taught me.

I believe that all carvers who write should explain – if only in a pen sketch – where their crucial and seminal influences come from, and how they learned their craft. In my own case I feel very pleased and privileged to be able to do so, such an impact did Gino have, both as a teacher and as a friend. When I dedicated my first book *Woodcarving Tools, Materials & Equipment* to him, it was an acknowledgement and an expression of gratitude; and when Gino Masero died in 1995 I was particularly glad to have done this while he could appreciate it.

The factor which unifies an understanding of the 'elements of woodcarving' into a confident, competent woodcarver is the mind and spirit which utilizes them. Once the basics are thoroughly absorbed, it is the individual mind, with its insights and aspirations, that separates one carver, one artist, from another, and has the potential to rise above mediocrity into something fresh and inspiring, no matter how modest.

This chapter is derived from two articles and a series of questions and answers which I wrote for *Woodcarving* magazine in 1994. I wrote them to celebrate a great enthusiast who embodied the craft of woodcarving. Having read them through, I feel I can add or change little. I am glad to include them in this book because the man really did understand, profoundly, what woodcarving was all about. His work and his observations provide many pointers to what is needed to master the art of woodcarving.

THE SHAPING OF A CARVER

Some time before he died, Gino Masero wrote an autobiography – 'largely for fun, for myself', as he put it – in which he 'documented the path whereby I entered and followed a lifelong love of woodcarving'. I had the great pleasure of reading the manuscript and extracted, with his kind permission, many of the following details and quotations from it.

When I first met Gino in 1975, several complementary qualities struck me: he was devoted to his craft; a great enthusiast for the work itself and for the woodcarving of others; and he was refreshingly humble, always willing to learn. Looking back at his life, the origins of these qualities – which together make for a fine carver – were not too hard to find.

Although born in Scarborough to a Yorkshire woman in 1915, he spent the first five years of his life in northern Italy with his father's farming family, returning to working-class London with little English. From somewhere in this mixture came the large, hard-working hands, the easy-going constitution that was interested in others but disliked pretension, the love of both art and nature, and a pride in his work that made him always strive to improve while simultaneously knowing his limits.

Gino showed a talent for carving as a boy, whittling potatoes into boats, which caused mashed potatoes to be common fare at home. His first attempts in wood were puppets for a toy theatre: witches, horses' heads and so on. Gino's description of his carving with a penknife is an education to newcomers to carving:

> Using a penknife it was difficult to round forms, so I simply had to be pleased with blocking them in with straight and angled cuts. It was a most important exercise as it made me simplify and look for easy planes. It was to develop into a shorthand method of carving which became invaluable in later years.

St Francis of Assisi in lime, 650mm (26in) high.
The carving expresses the joy of St Francis, singing and encouraging his companions

Although the creative urge was present from an early age and he excelled at drawing and modelling in school, when the time came to leave at 14 he had to start work in the hotel kitchen where his father was head chef. Since Gino's temperament was to give everything to what he undertook, he worked hard in those kitchens.

137

Then came one of those pivotal moments that are reminiscent of the best Hollywood films. In the hotel it was the practice to carve huge blocks of salt into deep, decorative dishes. Gino was given this job and turned out something spectacular: 'Two sturdy male figures knelt at each end of the bowl . . . drapery fell . . . the lip had flowers all around . . . ornamental grooves.' He was 15.

At this point it was obvious where Gino's heart and talents lay, and he started evening classes, supporting himself by working in the kitchens part time. During this important period he found release for pent-up energies in boxing:

> There was something in my character that responded to a challenge, especially if it was imaginative. If that were the case, an all-out effort would be made to see it through as best I could.

When tragedy struck a boxing friend, Gino decided to let the boxing go. He also left home to live on his own, and met his wife Kate.

The real watershed was a fortuitous meeting with the London carver Louis Dupuis, then aged 70, who became Gino Masero's first teacher:

> What a remarkable person he was, a small miracle had happened. They do at times and one has to recognize them when they occur. My spirits soared. Time and time again in my mind Monsieur Dupuis' instructions were gone over and over. I concentrated as never before. As far as I could see there were no major problems or setbacks. It was well within my power to learn the techniques of a special and ancient craft.

In token of the debt of gratitude one naturally feels toward one's first teacher, Gino repaid Louis many times by passing on the gift of teaching whenever there was an opportunity.

Gino began work first part time, then full time, as a frame carver, while still attending evening classes, visiting museums and aspiring higher. And after the last war – which saw Gino's talents being put to no recognizable use – his skill as a frame carver was of great benefit in repairing war damage.

In 1954 he completed, from design to execution, an elaborate set of 14 Stations of the Cross. Carved in his spare time, the panels were not only his first major solo carving, but also his first venture into figure carving. So successful was this work that on the strength of it Gino, then aged 39, was uprated to the status of a figure carver by the Carvers' Union; this was considered the highest level of the craft by most carvers, with the highest-rated earnings.

Then came the halcyon days for carvers, with post-war architectural restoration. He worked full time in a series of well-established, even prestigious architectural workshops in London (such as those of Robert Cross, E. J. & A. T. Bradford, and Graham and Groves) over many years, sharing benches with other very experienced carvers who became both friends and mentors.

> Architectural workshops . . . were grimy and could have done with several coats of paint . . . The ceilings were high. On the wall facing the windows hung dusty plaster casts of Corinthian caps, swags and drops, and a coat of arms. A few double and single Cherub heads peered blankly from odd positions, usually askew. Under each window benches were placed so as to get the maximum light possible . . . most of the benches had work attached with carving tools in convenient positions. Mallets were always in evidence, and so were strops. Also within reach were battered old tobacco tins that contained the slip stones for sharpening. On nails just above each bench were hung dividers and a calliper or two . . .

Working from a plaster model, Gino Masero carves a figure in the architectural workshop of Messrs Bradford and Son

In such establishments Gino Masero gained tremendous experience in all types of commercial carving: oak altarpieces, Gothic tracery, paterae, lettering, Chippendale mirrors, eagle and dolphin consoles, mouldings, figures and so on, as well as sculpture in stone.

Two notable pieces of work during this phase in Gino's career were the restoration of the overmantel by Grinling Gibbons (1648–1721) in the Old Admiralty Board Room, Whitehall, and restoration work in St Paul's Cathedral.

Most of the magnificent Gibbons overmantel had been reduced to so many boxes of bits by wartime bombing, and had to be reassembled. The many missing pieces needed replacing in the exact style and detail – a very exacting task calling for all the skills of a craftsman:

Gibbons had designed it with the sea in mind. Merchildren with lovely faces rode on dolphins, and bundles of hanging fish were entwined with long ropes of pearls. There were also his usual flamboyant festoons of fruit and flowers on the drops, as well as every kind of seashell. What was of particular interest, however, were various nautical instruments of the period which the master had introduced as an unusual decorative element. At the top centre of the overmantel were laurel leaves, with a crown, sword and trumpet. In the middle an Eye in Glory and, in the background, great Wings of Victory.

This work again led to a widening of experience and competence.

The work at St Paul's involved both stone and wood carving. A massive 2.4m (8ft) figure of Christ in gilded limewood, sculpted by Gino Masero, stands high above the main altar.

In 1964 he was elected a member of the prestigious Master Carvers Association. Then, as the amount of grand architectural carving began to decrease, Gino moved first into workshops of his own and eventually out of London altogether. From 1971 onwards he lived in Sussex, where he carved for a wide variety of clients. He was highly esteemed for the many heraldic devices he carved for the Royal College of Arms: coats of arms and crests for the Order of the Garter in Windsor, and for the Order of the Bath in Westminster Abbey.

Queen Anne's coat of arms. After being painted and gilded by a heraldic painter for the Royal College of Arms, it was forwarded to the USA

Head of Christ, based on the Turin Shroud: Quebec pine, 675mm (27in) high

One of several sketch carvings by Gino Masero of a samurai, about 300mm (12in) high, in jelutong. In this case the emphasis is on latent aggression

Gino Masero with his carving of Don Quixote de la Mancha

Beginning in 1975, shortly before I met him, Gino Masero continually taught evening classes, stopping at the age of 78. Right up until he died, he was still reassuringly vigorous (he always maintained that carvers were long-lived), and kept his hand and eye in by carving for relatives and friends in a workshop in the garden. The small work he produced, like his larger work, was an inspiration in design and technique to any carver. If he was right and carvers are long-lived, I for one take great reassurance in the hope that the years might allow me to approach the standard he set.

He saw himself as a trade carver, an honest workman practising and enjoying his skill to the best of his ability – which he truly did – and his background was definitely one of commercial woodcarving with its disciplines and its demand for both quality and speed. Yet the appreciations of Gino Masero's heart and mind were those of an artist, carving form with flair and precision.

LESSONS AT THE BENCH

When I visited Gino Masero in 1994 (when he was 79), I set him a problem. I had been intrigued by his description (quoted above) of his first carvings as a boy with a penknife. He describes himself blocking out forms in potatoes using straight and angled cuts, the tools and material making him simplify and look for easy planes. He has always taken this approach, getting into a carving quickly, and it seemed so fundamental that I thought it was worth exploring a little further.

So I inveigled Gino into his workshop one rainy afternoon, handed him a lump of wood and asked him, in the hour before teatime, to show me how he might rough out a simple face. I photographed it as he went along and made notes of the lessons to be learned. I think I lost count at about 30.

What I discovered exemplifies what I am trying to say in this book about the elements of design, technique and material coming together in the heart and mind of the carver.

But to start with he set *me* a problem: Gino was a carver with prodigious concentration, and I had to work quite hard, once he had started, to get him even to mumble at me. Perhaps indeed this was the first lesson: he concentrated, even when he was having a 'bit of fun' sketch-carving a face. The way he stood to the work showed that a large amount of his being was orientated to, even integrated with, what he was doing; he was not easily distracted. I myself was just as deeply involved in fiddling with the camera, so I could, in turn, only mutter things at Gino; and he would only mumble something back. Except for the gentle rain outside, the workshop was quiet, and as we muttered and mumbled all sorts of interesting considerations arose...

I should perhaps mention here that Gino was ambidextrous in carving, as all professional carvers are (or should be); the reason all the photographs show him working left-handed is simply that I was standing on his right, and there was no opportunity to change camera position while he worked.

It was a little unfair of me not to have specified what I wanted, which made it difficult for Gino to give it to me. So here was lesson 2: the more clearly you can see what you are aiming at – the clearer the idea in your mind – the better. This is why many carvers, especially in the architectural field, worked from clay or plaster models. The head that appears in these photographs should be seen as a quick doodle in the wood, with no model and no particular idea to work towards.

The next series of lessons involved his tools – and we'd hardly started yet. Gino had immaculately sharpened tools (and lots of them), and as the wood chips came away with a cool 'sspp!' sound, leaving a perfect, shiny surface, nothing more was needed.

CARVING

Gino's method of cutting involved a brisk, precise tool-stroke, across, with, and sometimes against the grain. It was a very workmanlike, no-nonsense approach, and quick. He would make a decision, then – *sspp!*

Gino also had two other admirable habits. Firstly, he worked with the widest possible tool at any time. This was especially so in the early stages, as you can see from Fig 13.4 onwards, where he rarely uses anything less than 25mm (1in) wide, apart from the V-tool. The second habit was to clean up the work as he went along – but more of that later. This must have been lesson 7 or thereabouts – let's go back to the beginning.

Gino Masero clamped the block firmly in the vice. His workshop had windows in the roof as well as the walls, which made for very good lighting. It was a nice piece of wood to start with: clear, tight, straight-grained lime. So here were three necessary ingredients for a good beginning to a carving: well-selected wood, held conveniently and securely, with good lighting to create working shadows.

Incidentally, Gino's bench came from an old East End furniture factory and had seen generations of work as a joiner's bench; like the man using it, it still functioned well, despite its age and condition!

Gino started by drawing a vertical centre line and a roughly head-shaped oval (Figs 13.1 and 13.2). The vertical line, redrawn when necessary, was a constant reference point. Even though in carving a face you are not aiming for perfect symmetry – what face has such a thing? – the line helps you achieve a believable degree of symmetry and a pleasing balance of features.

Gino then wasted away wood around the outline of the head with a large, deep gouge (Fig 13.3) and set in the shape with a large flat gouge. You can see, as we go along, how he regularly pushed the outlined shape further back into the wood. Next, he drew rough lines marking the position of the eyebrows and nose (Fig 13.4) and cut the corners away. A 13mm (½in) V-tool was used to run in the lower limit of the nose (Fig 13.5), and the same deep gouge then cut down the sides of the nose and into the eye sockets (Fig 13.6).

At this early stage, Gino was seeking out some of the main masses, the main forms and relationships, and was not afraid of making quite vigorous strokes. The chin started to appear (Fig 13.7), and a stroke with the V-tool set the position of the mouth (Fig 13.8). Gino then turned to pushing the side of the face away from the nose (Fig 13.9); a common fault with beginners is to make faces rather flat and not three-dimensional enough.

Two strokes of the V-tool (Fig 13.10), and the mouth appeared; two further cuts defined the wings of the nose (Fig 13.11).

Fig 13.3 Gino quickly cuts back the waste around the face, using the corner of the gouge to split off sizeable chunks

Fig 13.4 A rough outline to start, with eyebrow and nose positions marked

Fig 13.1 Without any preparation, Gino sketches an oval on the block of lime, held in the bench vice

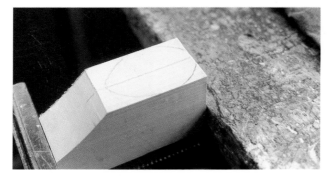

Fig 13.2 Ready to start: the centre line remains until the features are sufficiently fixed to ensure the necessary degree of symmetry

Fig 13.5 Using the V-tool to define the lower limit of the nose; forehead, cheeks and chin have been roughly bevelled off

Fig 13.6 *Nose and eye sockets are sketched in with a deep gouge*

Fig 13.9 *Cutting back the sides of the face and chin*

Fig 13.7 *The face so far: cheekbones and chin are beginning to emerge*

Fig 13.10 *The upper and lower lips are shaped with a large V-tool*

Fig 13.8 *The position of the mouth has been defined with the V-tool; now the sides of the face are taken back further*

Fig 13.11 *The wings of the nose are now appearing; the centre line is still present*

Fig 13.12 *Further work on the chin; note the continual cleanness of cutting*

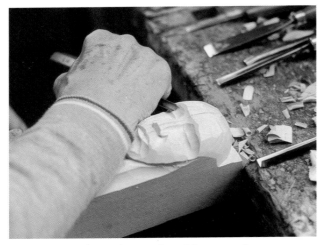

Fig 13.13 *Defining the muscles of the eye socket: a crucial moment*

Fig 13.14 *Working out where the eyes are to go*

Up to this point, Gino was trying 'to get down to the depths, while at the same time keeping the outline going'. The lesson about clean cutting is worth repeating here, as I repeat it elsewhere in this book: by continually cutting cleanly, the work naturally arrives at a finished state, and you can stop when you have had enough. There is no special cleaning-up stage, although a little tidying ('licking up') may be necessary. So the lesson is to *keep work as clean as possible, all the time*. You can see this in Fig 13.12, where the lower lip and chin are appearing.

Gino Masero was quietly working and feeling his way. One lovely moment came when he made a couple of cuts with a semicircular gouge to the eyes – and suddenly there was a face, waiting to be awoken (Fig 13.13).

Gino told me that at different moments he would find something, then lose it – he was trying to find something transient, to create a character, but couldn't quite determine what was wanted. I found this a very familiar observation – in woodcarving you are continuously cutting away what you are looking at. So here we had a lesson in exploration, keeping the form plastic and mobile, only slowly settling down and becoming fixed – bosting in, in fact. Figs 13.14–13.16 show this process of carving or seeking, which involves not a little risk-taking. To some extent this exploratory approach was inherent in the nature of the task that I had set Gino – and already we could hear the rattling of teacups. He was looking for something, but he did not really know what it was until he had found it.

Fig 13.15 *The face has been cut back further into the block, and the muscles above the eyes are beginning to appear*

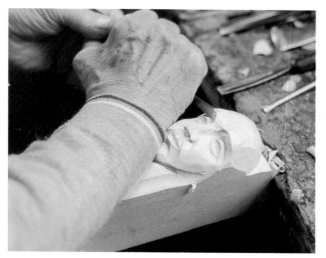

Fig 13.16 *Giving a little more definition to the eyebrow area*

Fig 13.17 *The hairline is in place; now the wings of the nose are being defined*

Fig 13.18 *A fishtail gouge sharpens the mouth crease and refines its shape*

Fig 13.19 *Placing the irises; the sides of the face have been taken further back*

The hairline went in next, and Gino pushed the outline of the head further back into the block of wood (Fig 13.17), all the time moving the whole piece along with crisp cuts to the mouth (Fig 13.18), side of the nose or eyebrows. Notice how Gino holds the fishtail gouge in this photograph. The last things to be carved were the eyes (Fig 13.19), leaving time for a little fiddling here and there and – time's up, tea's ready!

There is a lot of boldness in the facial features of the carving (Figs 13.20–13.22), and not a little of Gino's classical training; you can recognize the character of this sketch carving in his Madonna or Christ faces. Given time and clarity of intention, Gino Masero could create deeply felt and highly accomplished work; but you can still see in his finished pieces the vigorous, clean and purposeful cutting that is the vehicle for Gino Masero's vision.

Lessons over, all that remained was to clear up, thank Gino, and wend our way in for tea. I will end, though, with a moment of mumbling and muttering – in the quiet workshop, with the rain starting to hum on the roof and sharp edges of steel singing in the wood – the most revealing lesson of all:

GINO: 'We are really lucky people, we carvers, you know.'

ME: 'Say a bit more?'

GINO: 'Carving is a sort of joy, I think...'

Fig 13.20 *The sketch face given a coat of beeswax – seems contented enough!*

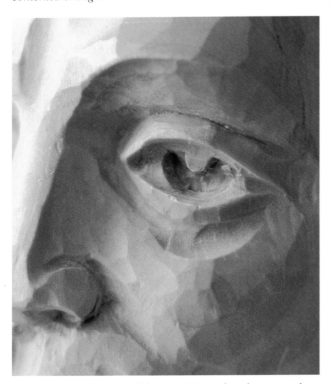

Fig 13.21 *A close-up of the eye. Remember this was only a quick sketch carving, never taken beyond the 'rough' stages; a more formal carving would be refined much further*

Fig 13.22 *Close-up of the mouth; note the defining groove on the lower lip, a classical touch which goes back beyond Greek carving to the Egyptians*

QUESTIONS

Gino's written replies to some of my questions were very revealing about his life, work and attitudes:

What work, now that you are retired, do you look back on as the most rewarding; and what has been the least?

Looking back over a lengthy working life, there were quite a few rewarding jobs – but there is no doubt in my mind that no carving could quite equal my first religious work. This was the Stations of the Cross, carved for our local church in Hampstead. The stations are a group of 14 scenes depicting Christ's Passion and Crucifixion, found in all Roman Catholic churches. In the early 1950s I was already qualified as a general carver, specializing in frame carving, but more than anything else I wanted to be a figure carver. There had always been this deep urge, nagging me to carve figures. The opportunity came almost as an answer to my prayers, but also as an enormous challenge: depicting the paradoxical suffering and dignity of the Christ figure. Each panel was about

24in [600mm] high, in French lime about 3in [75mm] thick. They took extensive research and preparatory work – there were eventually 63 figures in all. I carved them in the front room of my house in my spare time and, although I felt the last Station was more accomplished than the first, they were very well received. And as a result I was established as a figure carver by the Carvers' Union.

As to the least rewarding – well I must confess that I have always detested carving lengths of mouldings: the never-ending running patterns, from variations on Gothic vine leaves to Georgian ornament. After a bad session at the workshop I used to dream of logjams made up of hundreds of mouldings tumbling on to the bench. Of course, like everyone else I carved them – who couldn't? But one didn't have to like doing it.

It's a desert island; you get to take a piece of woodcarving, any size – which would you choose?

My one choice to while away the years of solitude on a desert island is easily selected: I would treasure and study that magnificent example of English seventeenth-century carving [by Grinling Gibbons] known as the Cosimo Panel. It measures 55 x 42in [1400 x 1070mm] and was sent as a gift to Cosimo III, Grand Duke of Tuscany, by Charles II in 1682.

May I hastily add to anyone facetious enough to enquire: No! I would not even consider using the panel as an improvised raft to get away from the island.

What in your view is the most important attitude a newcomer to carving could cultivate?

For me the answer can only be twofold: **commitment** and **tenacity**. A sincere and positive commitment of oneself to carving, plus the determination to hang on despite possible distractions and problems, which do occur at times.

Another helpful attitude to develop is one of humility: not only in coping with the onerous technical problems that confront novices, but also as they advance in the craft it enables them to select suitable subjects and ideas with which to further their advancing aims as carvers. Instructors do notice that many beginners tend to be a little ambitious in their choices.

What makes a 'good' woodcarving in your opinion, or a 'bad' one? And what makes a carving 'art' or 'sculpture'?

I feel that all 'good' carved work will be well designed for its purpose, on suitable and selected timber, cleanly cut with precision and care; and with all carving lines flowing and sweetly drawn with the appropriate carving tool. In finishing the piece, the shaping and surface modelling will be finalized with extremely sharp tools. When completed, the job should sparkle with interest, even giving off a little of that intangible joy a craftswoman or craftsman felt carving it.

A poor carving is a sorry thing: hesitant in execution, untidy and, worst of all, lifeless. Normally hacked with a few blunt chisels, in the first flush of creativity attempts are made – perhaps to some extent excusable – to solve the problem of poor toolwork on a torn and uneven surface, by rasping and sanding. This results in a plaster-like, smooth finish, and violates or desecrates a natural and lovely material in the process.

A flippant reply to the art and sculpture question must involve a load of building bricks, old iron, and a good agent. But more seriously, the criteria ought to be based on excellent technique, considerable study, creativity, and a great longing for beauty.

What are the commonest problems students have, and how do you help them?

Without doubt, the major problems that beset students initially are sharpening and using carving tools; and the difficulty of coping with the grain of the wood.

A counsel of perfection consists of continual 'one-to-one' demonstrations – preferably carried out by a competent tradesman, or a dedicated and qualified instructor. Failing this, study really intensively the very best primer on carving, and a video on the subject – I believe that a visual aid is very important to support bookwork.

Regarding the sharpening of carving tools, I must stress the need for razor-sharp chisels at all times. This cannot be reiterated often enough. No one can ever reach their full woodcarving potential without due attention to sharpening. It will pay dividends to anyone taking up the craft.

Japanese mask and woman's head: pierced relief in jelutong, about 770mm (28in) high

Celtic mask and woman's head: pierced relief in jelutong, about 770mm (28in) high

Medieval mask and woman's head: pierced relief in jelutong, about 770mm (28in) high

Detail of the Samurai carving in jelutong, shown in full on page 140

Amitabha Buddha in limewood, 400mm (16in) high, sitting on the windowsill of my workshop

Green Man: limewood, 380mm (15in) square

CHAPTER 14

TILMAN RIEMENSCHNEIDER

1460–1531

This chapter, like the last, was originally an article in *Woodcarving* magazine (1993); I include the material here as another exemplar of a carver who really brings together the 'elements of woodcarving' and raises them to much more than the sum of their parts. I do not want to draw any other parallel than this between Gino Masero and Tilman Riemenschneider; they lived very different lives, in different times, with different opportunities.

Riemenschneider is about as well known in English-speaking countries as Grinling Gibbons is in Germany – which is to say, not very well (although Gibbons has recently received some well-deserved attention in the Victoria and Albert Museum exhibition of 1998–9). This is not really surprising, as both men seem to occupy discrete niches in time and place, making them important individuals in a national rather than international sense.

Both worked to a startlingly high standard, but in completely separate styles, each producing a unique body of woodcarving. They both seem to have blossomed out of a peculiar fertility of their respective times and, in passing, left a bare branch which no other flowers can quite cover. We are left with a mere handful of exquisite petals (Fig 14.1).

A GOLDEN AGE

Tilman Riemenschneider was born in Heiligenstadt, in Eichsfeld, southern Germany, in 1460. His was a very full, broad and active life, most of which was spent in the same area, the Taubertal – the long valley of the River Tauber – and it is in this region (Fig 14.2) that his major remaining works can still be seen.

Fig 14.1 *The Heiligblut Altar (Altar of the Holy Blood) in St Jakob's Church, Rothenburg (built 1499–1505). Frame: pine; carving: limewood. An example of a retable or high altar extending to a height of 11m (36ft), with a central compartment containing figures, and carved doors which open to form the wings of the altar*

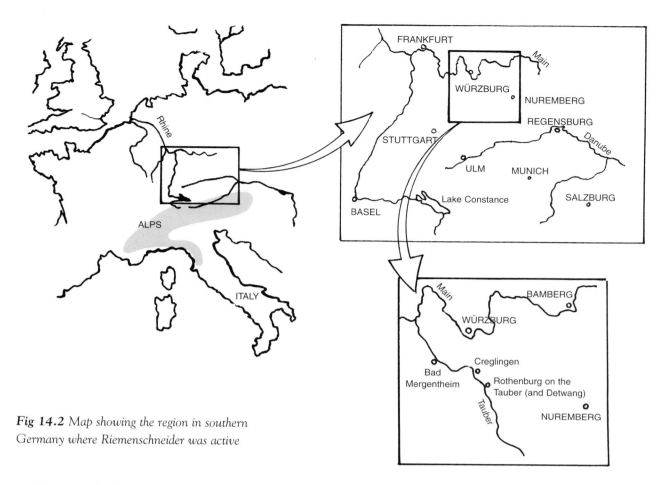

Fig 14.2 *Map showing the region in southern Germany where Riemenschneider was active*

The period of time into which Riemenschneider was born – particularly the 50 years or so between about 1480 and 1530 – witnessed a spectacular surge of creative energy among the wood sculptors and carvers of southern Germany. Contemporary with Riemenschneider were such illustrious figures as Veit Stoss, Michael Pacher and Michel and Gregor Ehrhart. In the fifteenth century, while the Italian Renaissance was getting into full swing, there was little interest north of the Alps in these rediscoveries of the classical past. Nevertheless, a parallel renaissance flourished, coloured by Gothic sensibilities. Often termed 'Late Gothic', this outstanding period is usually linked with the lifetime of Albrecht Dürer (1471–1528).

Sculpture up to this time was mostly in limestone, associated with cathedral workshops and physically inseparable from the building in which it appeared. As local towns began to grow, both in wealth and importance, the patronage of rich merchants and the clergy in the town councils promoted sculpture as an important means of signifying prestige and status. Suddenly carvings, predominantly in wood, became more self-contained and independent of their surroundings. Carvers were allowed greater freedom of expression and construction, while turning to one particular material to support their visions: limewood. This wood (also called linden) was initially abundant and cheap in the region. It could be shaped and worked in a very different way from the oak which had been so widely used earlier, and the use of limewood deeply affected the style and appearance of the new sculptural forms, which became looser, more fluid and open.

Most characteristic of the work being commissioned at the time is the *Hochaltar* or high altar (also known by the French name *retable*). This is a free-standing construction, often very complicated and sometimes up to 12m (40ft) high (see Fig 14.1 opposite). The central element of the high altar is a compartment like a large box, in which three-dimensional figures appear, as on a stage, for the sculptor to direct as part of a fully worked-out theme (Fig 14.3). A pair of doors, carved on the inside in complementary high relief, originally closed the box. Later, these doors were left wide open to form wings, designed to be seen as integral with the whole arrangement (Fig 14.4). The altar was an expression of the Catholic ideals of the time, and often included ebullient Gothic tracery and angels poised in flight (Fig 14.5). As a prestigious symbol, it more or less superseded the carving of single, isolated figures.

Several factors were important in bringing about this golden period of woodcarving in which Riemenschneider flourished: patronage, and the willingness to fund large projects; a deep tradition of carving out of which the artists arose to meet the demands of the moment; the isolation of southern Germany from the Italian Renaissance, which allowed it to develop a unique and peculiarly northern style; and limewood – a material which was fully exploited by the sculptors and which made these achievements possible. As some of these conditions changed, so the brief but golden age of Late Gothic genius came to an end.

Fig 14.4 *The right-hand wing of the Heiligblut Altar, showing Christ in the Garden of Gethsemane. The Passion of Christ was one of the major themes worked out in these retables*

Fig 14.3 *The central panel of the Heiligblut Altar, depicting the Last Supper. Riemenschneider's skill with perspective adds to the sense of drama*

Fig 14.5 *Detail from the Marienaltar (St Mary's Altar) in the Herrgottskirche, Creglingen (built 1505–10), showing an angel. Frame: pine, total height about 10m (33ft); carving: limewood*

THE LIFE

Tilman Riemenschneider himself is one of those larger-than-life characters: he was brilliant in his own creative work, innovative in design and in the way his material was worked. He was an entrepreneur and businessman with vast organizational skills, who ran a large and productive workshop. A politically active man, he acquired power and used it to his own, great, creative ends. And, lastly, he was a man whose social awareness and activity eventually led to his downfall and his somewhat tragic end.

Riemenschneider was born the son of a Müntzmeister – a master of coin minting – and was apprenticed in Würzburg as a woodcarver and stonemason. Of this period in his life, and the customary journeyman period which followed, nothing is known. In 1483, after his father died, he settled in Würzburg as a member of the Painters', Sculptors' and Glassmakers' Guild.

The guild system at that time was very strong and inward-looking, controlling among other things the mastership and membership of the guild – and thus who worked in the trade – the size of workshops, the number of apprentices, the supply of material, prices and quality, as well as the types and nature of the commissions undertaken.

In 1485 Tilman Riemenschneider made the first shrewd move of his career by marrying the widow of a master goldsmith. In keeping with the peculiarities of the guild system he acquired not only wealth but the status of *Meister* and the right to call himself a *Burger* – a position of fairly high status in those very rigidly class-conscious times.

This was the first of four marriages Riemenschneider made, each giving him greater wealth and influence. He moved upwards through a series of town-council positions, including head of town planning and building in Würzburg, which culminated in 1520 in his being elected town mayor. With this political leverage he was able to bend or circumvent guild practices and set up a large workshop with far more than the normal numbers of apprentices and journeymen. During a productive period of over 30 years his workshop created 19 known retable altars (Fig 14.6), as well as large numbers of carvings for less prestigious purposes, both in wood and stone. Quite likely his workshop also produced smaller 'off-the-shelf' pieces for more general consumption.

Fig 14.6 *Detail from the Marienaltar, Creglingen: the head of James the Elder, one of the figures gathered around the feet of Mary. Carving of great sensitivity captures an expression of entirely individual emotion*

His latter years were marked by great religious and social change throughout Europe. Martin Luther stayed in Würzburg and would probably have met Riemenschneider. Although Riemenschneider always remained a Catholic and was not a follower of Luther – he is shown holding a rosary on his tombstone – he spoke out against many of the social injustices of the time, advocating the abolition of many class and status privileges. In 1524 the 'Peasants' War' broke out in southern Germany, and a revolt of the peasantry in May 1525 ended in the occupation of Würzburg. The bishop, as the leading political figure, was expelled from Würzburg by the town council, of which Riemenschneider was a member. But in June that year the peasants were beaten and, with Würzburg retaken, the bishop returned to power. Contemporary documentary evidence tells how the burghers of Würzburg were taken prisoner and tried; some 65 were beheaded. Riemenschneider himself evaded this fate, but spent nine weeks in the prison of the Marienburg, the central fortress and palace of Würzburg. He was heavily fined and barred from holding a public position ever again. Worse, he is said to have been tortured and his hands broken; and, as if to support this assertion, no work that we know of ever came from those hands again.

Tilman Riemenschneider died in 1531, having just turned 70. A small figure in the predella (lower platform) of the Creglingen altar is almost certainly a self-portrait (Fig 14.7). It bears a striking similarity to the portrait of Riemenschneider on his tombstone, carved by his eldest son.

THE WORK

The size and enterprise of his workshop enabled a prodigious amount of woodcarving and sculpture to be produced, compared to the output of other contemporary carvers. Indeed, the incredible speed with which Riemenschneider completed his highly involved commissions points to a remarkably well-organized workshop team.

Because of his many other duties, Riemenschneider's role in the workshop must have been largely that of a supervisor, but there is no doubt

Fig 14.7 *This figure on the right-hand side of the predella of the Marienaltar in Creglingen is widely believed to be a self-portrait of Tilman Riemenschneider*

that he personally took on the most important carving. Quite often the difference between his hand and that of another can be seen: a work can be labelled 'after Riemenschneider' or 'Riemenschneider school', implying a conspicuous difference in quality of technique. He developed styles of drapery, form, posture and details such as eyes or beards that could be quickly and economically delegated to other carvers. These mannerisms are readily recognizable, and indeed they are one of the reasons why his work always seems so well at ease with the material (Figs 14.8 and 14.9).

His brilliant grasp of composition allowed him to make efficient use of the material. The particular qualities of limewood – its ability to take thin, sweeping forms and great detail, its tight structure allowing clean cutting across the grain – were fully exploited (Figs 14.10 and 14.11). Without the peculiar and unique qualities of this wood, such

Fig 14.8 *St Barbara: limewood, 1330mm (52in) high, in the Bayerisches Nationalmuseum, Munich; carved about 1515*

Fig 14.9 *Detail of the St Barbara. The gently curved posture, long nose and sloping, soulful eyes are characteristic of the carving of Tilman Riemenschneider, as is the economic cutting of the hair and mouth. Only the eyes may have been coloured*

Fig 14.10 *The Elevation of the Magdalene: limewood, 1860mm (73in) high; Bayerisches Nationalmuseum, Munich. Carved around 1490–2 as part of a retable for a church in Münnerstadt, but taken to pieces during the Baroque period and now dispersed in various museums*

Fig 14.11 *Detail of the Magdalene. The sheer fluidity of the hair is phenomenal, and calls for the highest ability in handling carving tools*

155

adventurous cutting and designing could not have taken place; it is an interesting idea that, without the lime tree, this Late Gothic renaissance could not have occurred.

Working practice involved single- and double-bevelled axes, adzes and drills for preliminary roughing out; woodcuts of the time show that individual figures were carved horizontally rather than upright. Skew chisels and knives created the details. Sometimes parts were abraded to provide areas of contrast. The limewood was hardly seasoned at all when carving began, and to allow for the movement of drying without splitting, the bulkier masses were hollowed out at the back.

Riemenschneider's work is characterized by swathes of drapery executed with great flair (Fig 14.12). The faces he carved are full of pathos and deep emotion, even though they came from such an industrious workshop.

Up to this time, all sculpture was polychromed, and the bright colours and gilding applied to a gessoed surface necessitated a coarser style of carving to support the final details. This approach can be seen in the earlier work of Veit Stoss, for example. The painting was carried out by specialists, and with all the artisans belonging to the same guild, projects often became complicated and frustrating. Tilman Riemenschneider was a major mover in overriding guild restrictions, and one of the first to produce unpainted sculptures. A change in public taste from about 1490 allowed the limewood to be finished with only a thin, pigmented glaze, which permitted sculptural details to be more finely cut (Fig 14.13).

Tilman Riemenschneider is important not only because he was a fine carver in his own right, with designs perfectly fitting the material he was working with, but also because the large output of his workshop over 40 years – both in wood and stone – influenced many journeymen carvers throughout the surrounding area. Of the 19 known high altars or retables that Tilman Riemenschneider created – some for quite small parish churches – only two survive *in situ*. The Heiligblut Altar in St Jakob's Church, Rothenburg on the Tauber was created between 1499 and 1505 (see Fig 14.1 on page 150), and in the Herrgottskirche in Creglingen can be seen the Marienaltar, made

Fig 14.12 Detail of one of the angels accompanying the Magdalene: unrestrained drapery evokes movement. This ebullience comes from the material: limewood allows for great freedom of design. The simple cutting of the fringe enhances the bouncing curves

Fig 14.13 Detail of the St Barbara (see Fig 14.8). Notice how light and sensitive is the treatment of the hands

between 1505 and 1510 (see Fig 14.5 on page 152). These two retables can be seen today, well cared for and sympathetically lit; they show all the virtuosity of the man. Many other figures from larger structures survive in museums in Germany, and these are also well worth visiting and pondering over.

With the Reformation, and all-consuming time, much of Tilman Riemenschneider's work has been destroyed or lost. From the 1520s the demand for the great carved altars diminished, partly due to the 'anti-figurative' tone of the Reformation, and partly because patrons lost their confidence in the future. Another factor was the increasing interest of Germanic artists in antiquity and the arrival of the newer, and more fashionable, Italian Renaissance style. So the golden age closed with sculptors adapting the public, monumental style of their work to a smaller scale and a more private audience, and moving away from limewood to even more intricate work in boxwood and pearwood.

WHERE TO SEE THE WORK OF TILMAN RIEMENSCHNEIDER

In the UK there are only three examples of his work, all in the Victoria and Albert Museum in London, and even some of these may be 'off-the-shelf' carvings by members of his workshop. A bust of St Bukard (1510) is housed in the National Gallery, Washington, DC.

Otherwise, to see the work of Tilman Riemenschneider requires a pilgrimage to southern Germany – which is well worth doing. Besides the two major retables at Rothenburg and Creglingen, a smaller altar is to be seen at Detwang, just outside Rothenburg. There are many isolated figures and panels in wood and stone – parts of what were once composite pieces – in both the Mainfrankisches Museum in Würzburg and the Bayerisches Nationalmuseum in Munich. A few other carvings can be seen in museums in Berlin and Nuremberg.

A PERSONAL NOTE

Words and pictures are not enough. Anyone who has attempted to carve, even at the simplest level, will soon understand what makes Tilman Riemenschneider among the greatest of all woodcarvers; you only have to stand in front of one of the remaining high altars at Creglingen or Rothenburg, or the large single figures in the museums of Würzburg or Munich, and look, and feel. To a carver especially, the technical mastery, the plasticity of form and the overall conception of the designs are astonishing; and the sheer emotional weight leaves one a little breathless and awestruck.

A TIME FRAME OF EVENTS DURING THE LIFE OF TILMAN RIEMENSCHNEIDER

- 1475 Caxton introduces printing to England

- 1484 Pope Innocent VIII declares witchcraft a heresy

- 1492 Columbus lands in the West Indies

- 1501–4 Michelangelo carves the *David*

- 1503 Leonardo da Vinci paints the *Mona Lisa*

- 1509 Henry VIII enthroned

- 1517 Luther nails his 95 Theses to the church door at Wittenberg

- 1522 Magellan's expedition circumnavigates the globe

- 1523 Cortés overthrows the Aztec empire

- 1529 Siege of Vienna marks Islam's furthest point of conquest

METRIC CONVERSION TABLE

INCHES TO MILLIMETRES

inches	mm	inches	mm	inches	mm
⅛	3	9	229	30	762
¼	6	10	254	31	787
⅜	10	11	279	32	813
½	13	12	305	33	838
⅝	16	13	330	34	864
¾	19	14	356	35	889
⅞	22	15	381	36	914
1	25	16	406	37	940
1¼	32	17	432	38	965
1½	38	18	457	39	991
1¾	44	19	483	40	1016
2	51	20	508	41	1041
2½	64	21	533	42	1067
3	76	22	559	43	1092
3½	89	23	584	44	1118
4	102	24	610	45	1143
4½	114	25	635	46	1168
5	127	26	660	47	1194
6	152	27	686	48	1219
7	178	28	711	49	1245
8	203	29	737	50	1270

ABOUT THE AUTHOR

Chris Pye has been carving professionally for over 25 years, and owes his formative start to the master carver Gino Masero. His work is done mainly to commission, and ranges from architectural to figure carving; his repertoire includes furniture, lettering, bedheads, fireplaces and abstract sculpture.

He has taught local and residential woodcarving classes in England for many years, and is also a member of the faculty at the Center for Furniture Craftsmanship in Maine, USA, where he runs carving courses each year.

He is the author of *Woodcarving Tools, Materials & Equipment* (1994), *Carving on Turning* (1995), *Lettercarving in Wood: A Practical Course* (1997) and *Relief Carving in Wood: A Practical Introduction* (1998), all published by GMC Publications.

Chris Pye has written and runs a website (http://www.chrispye-woodcarving.com) dedicated to the teaching, learning and love of woodcarving, from which he edits the interactive journal *Slipstone*.

He lives in rural Herefordshire with his wife Karin Vogel and son Finian. His older son Daniel has a degree in art.

Chris Pye
The Poplars
Ewyas Harold
Hereford HR2 0HU

Email: chrispye@woodcarver.f9.co.uk

INDEX

WOODCARVING

Beginning Woodcarving	*GMC Publications*
Carving Architectural Detail in Wood: The Classical Tradition	*Frederick Wilbur*
Carving Birds & Beasts	*GMC Publications*
Carving the Human Figure: Studies in Wood and Stone	*Dick Onians*
Carving Nature: Wildlife Studies in Wood	*Frank Fox-Wilson*
Carving on Turning	*Chris Pye*
Celtic Carved Lovespoons: 30 Patterns	*Sharon Littley & Clive Griffin*
Decorative Woodcarving (New Edition)	*Jeremy Williams*
Elements of Woodcarving	*Chris Pye*
Essential Woodcarving Techniques	*Dick Onians*
Figure Carving in Wood: Human and Animal Forms	*Sara Wilkinson*
Lettercarving in Wood: A Practical Course	*Chris Pye*
Relief Carving in Wood: A Practical Introduction	*Chris Pye*
Woodcarving for Beginners	*GMC Publications*
Woodcarving Made Easy	*Cynthia Rogers*
Woodcarving Tools, Materials & Equipment (New Edition in 2 vols.)	*Chris Pye*

WOODTURNING

Bowl Turning Techniques Masterclass	*Tony Boase*
Chris Child's Projects for Woodturners	*Chris Child*
Contemporary Turned Wood: New Perspectives in a Rich Tradition	
	Ray Leier, Jan Peters & Kevin Wallace
Decorating Turned Wood: The Maker's Eye	*Liz & Michael O'Donnell*
Green Woodwork	*Mike Abbott*
Intermediate Woodturning Projects	*GMC Publications*
Keith Rowley's Woodturning Projects	*Keith Rowley*
Making Screw Threads in Wood	*Fred Holder*
Segmented Turning: A Complete Guide	*Ron Hampton*
Turned Boxes: 50 Designs	*Chris Stott*
Turning Green Wood	*Michael O'Donnell*
Turning Pens and Pencils	*Kip Christensen & Rex Burningham*
Woodturning: Forms and Materials	*John Hunnex*
Woodturning: A Foundation Course (New Edition)	*Keith Rowley*
Woodturning: A Fresh Approach	*Robert Chapman*
Woodturning: An Individual Approach	*Dave Regester*
Woodturning: A Source Book of Shapes	*John Hunnex*
Woodturning Masterclass	*Tony Boase*
Woodturning Techniques	*GMC Publications*

WOODWORKING

Beginning Picture Marquetry	*Lawrence Threadgold*
Celtic Carved Lovespoons: 30 Patterns	*Sharon Littley & Clive Griffin*
Celtic Woodcraft	*Glenda Bennett*
Complete Woodfinishing (Revised Edition)	*Ian Hosker*
David Charlesworth's Furniture-Making Techniques	*David Charlesworth*
David Charlesworth's Furniture-Making Techniques – Volume 2	*David Charlesworth*
Furniture-Making Projects for the Wood Craftsman	*GMC Publications*
Furniture-Making Techniques for the Wood Craftsman	*GMC Publications*
Furniture Projects with the Router	*Kevin Ley*
Furniture Restoration (Practical Crafts)	*Kevin Jan Bonner*
Furniture Restoration: A Professional at Work	*John Lloyd*
Furniture Restoration and Repair for Beginners	*Kevin Jan Bonner*
Furniture Restoration Workshop	*Kevin Jan Bonner*
Green Woodwork	*Mike Abbott*
Intarsia: 30 Patterns for the Scrollsaw	*John Everett*
Kevin Ley's Furniture Projects	*Kevin Ley*
Making Chairs and Tables – Volume 2	*GMC Publications*
Making Classic English Furniture	*Paul Richardson*
Making Heirloom Boxes	*Peter Lloyd*
Making Screw Threads in Wood	*Fred Holder*
Making Woodwork Aids and Devices	*Robert Wearing*
Mastering the Router	*Ron Fox*
Pine Furniture Projects for the Home	*Dave Mackenzie*
Router Magic: Jigs, Fixtures and Tricks to Unleash your Router's Full Potential	*Bill Hylton*
Router Projects for the Home	*GMC Publications*

Router Tips & Techniques	*Robert Wearing*
Routing: A Workshop Handbook	*Anthony Bailey*
Routing for Beginners	*Anthony Bailey*
Sharpening: The Complete Guide	*Jim Kingshott*
Space-Saving Furniture Projects	*Dave Mackenzie*
Stickmaking: A Complete Course	*Andrew Jones & Clive George*
Stickmaking Handbook	*Andrew Jones & Clive George*
Storage Projects for the Router	*GMC Publications*
Veneering: A Complete Course	*Ian Hosker*
Veneering Handbook	*Ian Hosker*
Woodworking Techniques and Projects	*Anthony Bailey*
Woodworking with the Router: Professional Router Techniques any Woodworker can Use	*Bill Hylton & Fred Matlack*

UPHOLSTERY

Upholstery: A Complete Course (Revised Edition)	*David James*
Upholstery Restoration	*David James*
Upholstery Techniques & Projects	*David James*
Upholstery Tips and Hints	*David James*

TOYMAKING

Scrollsaw Toy Projects	*Ivor Carlyle*
Scrollsaw Toys for All Ages	*Ivor Carlyle*

DOLLS' HOUSES AND MINIATURES

1/12 Scale Character Figures for the Dolls' House	*James Carrington*
Americana in 1/12 Scale: 50 Authentic Projects	*Joanne Ogreenc & Mary Lou Santovec*
The Authentic Georgian Dolls' House	*Brian Long*
A Beginners' Guide to the Dolls' House Hobby	*Jean Nisbett*
Celtic, Medieval and Tudor Wall Hangings in 1/12 Scale Needlepoint	*Sandra Whitehead*
Creating Decorative Fabrics: Projects in 1/12 Scale	*Janet Storey*
Dolls' House Accessories, Fixtures and Fittings	*Andrea Barham*
Dolls' House Furniture: Easy-to-Make Projects in 1/12 Scale	*Freida Gray*
Dolls' House Makeovers	*Jean Nisbett*
Dolls' House Window Treatments	*Eve Harwood*
Edwardian-Style Hand-Knitted Fashion for 1/12 Scale Dolls	*Yvonne Wakefield*
How to Make Your Dolls' House Special: Fresh Ideas for Decorating	*Beryl Armstrong*
Making 1/12 Scale Wicker Furniture for the Dolls' House	*Sheila Smith*
Making Miniature Chinese Rugs and Carpets	*Carol Phillipson*
Making Miniature Food and Market Stalls	*Angie Scarr*
Making Miniature Gardens	*Freida Gray*
Making Miniature Oriental Rugs & Carpets	*Meik & Ian McNaughton*
Making Miniatures: Projects for the 1/12 Scale Dolls' House	*Christiane Berridge*
Making Period Dolls' House Accessories	*Andrea Barham*
Making Tudor Dolls' Houses	*Derek Rowbottom*
Making Upholstered Furniture in 1/12 Scale	*Janet Storey*
Making Victorian Dolls' House Furniture	*Patricia King*
Medieval and Tudor Needlecraft: Knights and Ladies in 1/12 Scale	*Sandra Whitehead*
Miniature Bobbin Lace	*Roz Snowden*
Miniature Crochet: Projects in 1/12 Scale	*Roz Walters*
Miniature Embroidery for the Georgian Dolls' House	*Pamela Warner*
Miniature Embroidery for the Tudor and Stuart Dolls' House	*Pamela Warner*
Miniature Embroidery for the 20th-Century Dolls' House	*Pamela Warner*
Miniature Embroidery for the Victorian Dolls' House	*Pamela Warner*
Miniature Needlepoint Carpets	*Janet Granger*
More Miniature Oriental Rugs & Carpets	*Meik & Ian McNaughton*
Needlepoint 1/12 Scale: Design Collections for the Dolls' House	*Felicity Price*
New Ideas for Miniature Bobbin Lace	*Roz Snowden*
Patchwork Quilts for the Dolls' House: 20 Projects in 1/12 Scale	*Sarah Williams*
Simple Country Furniture Projects in 1/12 Scale	*Alison J. White*

CRAFTS

Bargello: A Fresh Approach to Florentine Embroidery	*Brenda Day*
Beginning Picture Marquetry	*Lawrence Threadgold*
Blackwork: A New Approach	*Brenda Day*
Celtic Cross Stitch Designs	*Carol Phillipson*

MAGAZINES

WOODTURNING · WOODCARVING
FURNITURE & CABINETMAKING
THE ROUTER · NEW WOODWORKING
THE DOLLS' HOUSE MAGAZINE
OUTDOOR PHOTOGRAPHY
BLACK & WHITE PHOTOGRAPHY
TRAVEL PHOTOGRAPHY
MACHINE KNITTING NEWS
KNITTING
GUILD OF MASTER CRAFTSMEN NEWS

The above represents a selection of titles currently published or scheduled to be published.
All are available direct from the Publishers or through bookshops, newsagents and specialist retailers.
To place an order, or to obtain a complete catalogue, contact:

GMC Publications,
166 High Street Lewes East Sussex BN7 1XU United Kingdom
Tel: 01273 488005 Fax: 01273 478606

Orders by credit card are accepted